Bad Breaks in Real GDP and Employment

"In an era when the marginal cost of conducting various statistical tests has approached zero, an alarmingly large proportion of empirical work is less a test among competing hypotheses than an illustration that the data can be made to confess if tortured sufficiently. Hartman's refreshing book represents a break from this trend as he leaves us with many puzzles in the data which deserve attention if we are to advance current thinking. It will be fertile ground for emerging scholars ready to plow new ground."

—Raymond E. Lombra, *Emeritus Professor of Economics and Former Associate Dean, Penn State University, Former Senior Staff Economist, Board of Governors of the Federal Reserve System*

Harrison C. Hartman

Bad Breaks in Real GDP and Employment

Exploring the Persistence of Aggregate Demand Shocks in the United States

palgrave
macmillan

Harrison C. Hartman
Rehoboth Beach, Delaware, USA

ISBN 978-3-031-57768-0 ISBN 978-3-031-57769-7 (eBook)
https://doi.org/10.1007/978-3-031-57769-7

This Palgrave Macmillan imprint is published by the registered company Springer Nature Switzerland AG
The registered company address is: Gewerbestrasse 11, 6330 Cham, Switzerland

Paper in this product is recyclable.

For Christopher R., Dolores M., and Harrison G.

Acknowledgments

I gratefully acknowledge the help and encouragement of my family, particularly my parents Harrison G. and Dolores M. and my brother Christopher. I also am thankful for my editor, Bronwyn Geyer and others at Palgrave Macmillan, for believing in this project and publishing this book. Additionally, I would like to thank Ray Lombra and Norman Swanson for answering my questions and/or reading drafts of material. Thanks also go to two anonymous referees. Further, I want to thank people at conferences for discussing material with me and answering questions. I also want to thank all of the teachers and professors who have influenced my teaching, research, writing, and life. Thanks also to the authors whose works are cited.

Please do not blame any of the above named people or others for any of the content in this book. After all, it is not their book! Also, thanks to you, the readers!

About This Book

The book that you are now reading presents econometric evidence both supporting the view and contradicting the view that some decreases in aggregate demand have had essentially permanent negative consequences for subsequent U.S. real GDP data. In contrast to mainstream macroeconomic theory, much if not most of the evidence in this book supports the view. My understanding is that few books that draw such conclusions offer extensive supporting econometric analysis.

As with my first book, *caveat emptor*! Because of the potential significance, I want to make the results which may be tentative available as soon as possible. You agree that neither I nor the Publisher will be liable for damages that you may incur from reading this book. Please refer to harrisonhartman.blogspot.com or the Palgrave Macmillan website or search 'Harrison C. Hartman' (perhaps with 'economics' or 'macroeconomics') for the appendix and updates, extensions, and corrections and/or instructions on where to find such information. Also, please realize that the appendix will probably be online only and that it may be 'under construction' when the book is published. Further, please realize that a citation does *not* necessarily mean that I have read or agree with a work.

Contents

1 Introduction to Modern Mainstream Macroeconomic Thought Versus Keynes' Views on Recoveries from Recessions 1

1.1 Overview of Classical, Monetarist, and Mainstream Modern Keynesian Analysis 2

1.2 Keynes' View on Full Employment in The General Theory of Employment, Interest, and Money 8

1.3 A Brief Overview of This Book 9

References 10

2 Literature Review of Major Schools of Macroeconomic Thought and Empirical Work 11

2.1 A Brief Introduction 12

2.2 Schools of Macroeconomic Thought 12

2.3 Econometric Work Related to the Duration of Negative Aggregate Demand Shocks 22

References 28

3 Results from Estimating and Projecting Trends for Recent Recessions 31

3.1 Introductory Comments 32

3.2 The Great Recession 33

3.3 The Dot-Com-Bubble Recession 47

3.4 Recap and Preparatory Remarks for the Next Chapter 53
References 58

4 Econometric Issues To Consider and Model Selection for Some Hypothesis Tests 59
4.1 Brief Recap of Results from Previous Chapters and Introduction to the Current Chapter 60
4.2 Standard Regression Assumptions 61
4.3 Some Notes About Testing with Data in First Difference Form 64
4.4 Model Selection, Differencing, and a Caveat 66
References 69

5 Hypothesis Testing with Real GDP: Somewhat Mixed Results 71
5.1 Chow Breakpoint Testing 72
5.2 Wald Restriction Tests and t*-Tests of Intercept Terms* 78
5.3 Chow Forecast Test Results 84
5.4 Testing for a Unit Root with a Break: Tentative Results 85
5.5 Brief Summary of Results from Testing for Breaks 93
References 94

6 Derived Demand for Labor and Breaks in Trend: Does Hysteresis in Employment Imply Hysteresis in the Growth Path of Real Output? 95
6.1 The Demand for Labor and a Very Brief Description of U.S. Nonfarm Payroll Employment—A Nonstationary Series 96
6.2 Breakpoint Unit Root Testing for U.S. Nonfarm Payroll Employment 99
6.3 Chow Breakpoint Testing for U.S. Nonfarm Payroll Employment 102
6.4 Summary of Results from Testing for Employment Breaks and Preparation for the Final Chapter 105
References 106

7 Similar Results from an Extended Sample Period and Concluding Remarks to Guide Future Work 107
7.1 Introduction and an Extended Sample Period with a Simple Method for Estimating Trend 108

7.2 Breakpoint Unit Root Testing with an Extended Sample Period 112
7.3 Chow Breakpoint Testing with an Extended Sample Period and a Brief Recap 116
7.4 Book Summary to This Point 119
7.5 Thoughts about the Importance of and Explanations for the Results and Future Work 122
References 128

Index 129

About the Author

Dr. Harrison C. Hartman author of approximately fifteen refereed journal publications, earned his BA, MA, and PhD in economics from Penn State University. He also earned an MBA from Saint Joseph's University. Before most recently teaching at Emory University, Harrison also taught at Georgia State University. Prior to that, Harrison won teaching awards at the University of Georgia. He also taught at Kennesaw State University, Ursinus College, and Penn State University, the last of which while still a student there in graduate school.

Bad Breaks (short title) is his second book. Harrison is enjoying his return to Pennsylvania. Find out more about Harrison at his X (formerly twitter) account (@HarrisonCHartm1) and his blog harrison-hartman.blogspot.com, the latter of which will have an online appendix for this book or instructions on where to find the online appendix or both.

List of Figures

Fig. 3.1	Quarterly data for the natural log of U.S. real GDP, annualized and seasonally adjusted, and the trend of the natural log of U.S. real GDP from the first quarter of 1947 through the second quarter of 2016 (*Sources* www.economagic.com, U.S. Bureau of Economic Analysis, Saint Louis Federal Reserve Bank, and the author's calculations)	34
Fig. 3.2	Relationship between U.S. real GDP in natural log form, its estimated trend (both in the top set of axes) and the estimated gap variable with the trend estimated from the first quarter of 1947 through the second quarter of 2016 (*Sources* www.economagic.com, U.S. Bureau of Economic Analysis, Saint Louis Federal Reserve Bank, and the author's calculations)	35
Fig. 3.3	Estimated 'gap variables' from the first quarter of 2000 through the second quarter of 2016 showing the actual natural log of quarterly U.S. real GDP (annualized and seasonally adjusted) minus its estimated trend with the trend estimated using observations (1) from the first quarter of 1947 through the second quarter of 2016 (GAP_47Q1_16Q2), (2) from the first quarter of 1947 through the fourth quarter of 2007 (GAP_47Q1_07Q4), and (3) from the first quarter of 2001 through the fourth quarter of 2007 (GAP_01Q1_07Q4) (*Sources* www.economagic.com, U.S. Bureau of Economic Analysis, Saint Louis Federal Reserve Bank, and the author's calculations)	41

Fig. 3.4 Quarterly data for the natural log of U.S. per capita real GDP, annualized and seasonally adjusted, and the trend of the natural log of U.S. per capita real GDP from the first quarter of 1947 through the second quarter of 2016 (*Sources* Saint Louis Federal Reserve Bank FRED web page, U.S. Bureau of Economic Analysis, and the author's calculations) 42
Fig. 3.5 Estimated 'gap variables' from the first quarter of 2000 through the second quarter of 2016 showing the actual natural log of quarterly U.S. per capita real GDP (annualized and seasonally adjusted) minus its estimated trend with the trend estimated using observations (1) from the first quarter of 1947 through the second quarter of 2016 (PC_GAP_47Q1_16Q2), (2) from the first quarter of 1947 through the fourth quarter of 2007 (PC_GAP_47Q1_07Q4), (3) from the first quarter of 2001 through the fourth quarter of 2007 (PC_GAP_01Q1_07Q4), and (4) from the third quarter of 2000 through the fourth quarter of 2007 (PC_GAP_00Q3_07Q4) (*Sources* Saint Louis Federal Reserve Bank FRED web page, U.S. Bureau of Economic Analysis, and the author's calculations) 45
Fig. 3.6 Estimated 'gap variables' from the first quarter of 2000 through the second quarter of 2016 showing the actual natural log of quarterly U.S. real GDP (annualized and seasonally adjusted) minus its estimated trend with the trend estimated using observations (1) from the first quarter of 1947 through the fourth quarter of 2000 (GAP_47Q1_00Q4), (2) from the third quarter of 1990 through the fourth quarter of 2000 (GAP_90Q3_00Q4), and (3) from the fourth quarter of 1990 through the fourth quarter of 2000 (GAP_90Q4_00Q4) (*Sources* www.economagic.com, U.S. Bureau of Economic Analysis, Saint Louis Federal Reserve Bank, and the author's calculations) 50
Fig. 3.7 Estimated 'gap variables' from the first quarter of 2000 through the second quarter of 2016 showing the actual natural log of quarterly U.S. per capita real GDP (annualized and seasonally adjusted) minus its estimated trend with the trend estimated using observations (1) from the first quarter of 1947 through the fourth quarter of 2000 (PC_GAP_47Q1_00Q4), (2) from the third quarter of 1990 through the fourth quarter of 2000 (PC_GAP_90Q3_00Q4), and (3) from the fourth quarter of 1990 through the fourth quarter of 2000 (PC_GAP_90Q4_00Q4) (*Sources* Saint Louis Federal Reserve Bank FRED web page, U.S. Bureau of Economic Analysis, and the author's calculations) 52

Fig. 6.1 The natural log of monthly U.S. nonfarm payroll employment (in thousands), January 1939 through December 2017 (*Sources* U.S. Bureau of Labor Statistics, Saint Louis Federal Reserve Bank FRED web page, and the author's calculations) 98

List of Tables

Table 3.1	Summary of results for U.S. recessions as defined in this book from the recession of 1949 through the Great Recession as to whether the natural logs of total U.S. real GDP and per capita U.S. real GDP returned to their pre-recession trends before the next recession (or by the second quarter of 2016 in the case of the Great Recession)	57
Table 3.2	Approximate values of the constant term (or the intercept) and the coefficient for the time trend over various selected time spans estimated to calculate gap variables for the dot-com-bubble recession and the Great Recession	58
Table 4.1	Summary of regression results of the two models over the full sample period	68
Table 5.1	Chow breakpoint test *p*-value results for multiple breaks in the constant in each test using the *F*-test and the Wald statistic for both Model A (total real GDP) and Model B (per capita real GDP)	74
Table 5.2	Additional Chow breakpoint test *p*-value results (with alternate sets of quarters, in many cases, not-recession-initiating) for multiple breaks in the constant in each test using the *F*-test and the Wald statistics for both Model A (total real GDP) and Model B (per capita real GDP)	75
Table 5.3	Regression results for Set 2 (with dummy variables for breaks in the third quarter of 1953, the first quarter of 2001, and the first quarter of 2008) using Model A (with the change in total real GDP)	78

Table 5.4 The time-varying function determining the change in the natural log of total real GDP in the U.S. implied by the results for Set 2 in Table 5.1 79

Table 5.5 Wald Coefficient Restriction test *p*-values for Chi-squared statistics 81

Table 5.6 Selected breakpoint unit root test results for the natural log of total U.S. real GDP 90

Table 5.7 Selected breakpoint unit root test results for the natural log of per capita U.S. real GDP 92

Table 6.1 Breakpoint unit root test results for the natural log of total U.S. nonfarm payroll employment, January 1939 through December 2017 101

Table 6.2 Chow breakpoint tests for two joint breaks in January 1953 and May 2000 in the intercepts of the equations for the change in the natural log of total U.S. nonfarm payroll employment 104

Table 7.1 Estimates of the intercept and the trend coefficient in equations for the natural log of real U.S. GDP, either in total or per capita, as a function of an intercept and a time trend multiplied by a coefficient 109

Table 7.2 Selected estimated values of (data likely revised for) the actual natural log of real GDP minus its trend for both total U.S. real GDP and per capita U.S. real GDP (Per Cap) in the fourth quarter of 2007, the second quarter of 2016, and the fourth quarter of 2019 110

Table 7.3 Selected breakpoint unit root test results for the natural log of total U.S. real GDP 113

Table 7.4 Selected breakpoint unit root test results for the natural log of per capita U.S. real GDP 115

Table 7.5 Chow breakpoint test results for multiple breaks in the intercepts of equations for the first difference in the natural log of either total U.S. real GDP or per capita U.S. real GDP using the indicated sets of quarters 118

CHAPTER 1

Introduction to Modern Mainstream Macroeconomic Thought Versus Keynes' Views on Recoveries from Recessions

Abstract An introductory chapter, this chapter offers brief overviews of three of the major schools of macroeconomic thought to provide some context for this book. Regarding the major schools of thought, this chapter focuses on the classical school of thought, the Keynesian school of thought, and the monetarist school of thought. With an emphasis on how decreases in aggregate demand could cause downward breaks in U.S. real GDP and employment, this book would best be categorized in the Keynesian school of thought. In contrast to mainstream macroeconomic theory, this chapter also discusses Keynes' view in *The General Theory of Employment, Interest, and Money* where economies could reach equilibrium at less than full employment and remain there for longer than the short term. Additionally, this chapter offers a short overview of the remainder of the book.

Keywords Keynesian school of macroeconomic thought · Monetarist school of macroeconomic thought · Classical school of monetarist thought · Keynes · Macroeconomics · GDP · Aggregate demand · Breaks in trend · Employment

H. C. Hartman, *Bad Breaks in Real GDP and Employment*,
https://doi.org/10.1007/978-3-031-57769-7_1

1.1 Overview of Classical, Monetarist, and Mainstream Modern Keynesian Analysis

This book offers an overview of how mainstream macroeconomic theories view recoveries from recessions and some challenges to the mainstream perspectives. Data from the U.S. economy in recent decades provides opportunities to get a sense of how applicable different viewpoints are in describing post-recession experiences, with emphasis placed on the U.S. economy. Loosely speaking, aggregate demand refers to the total value of domestically made items that various categories of customers, including government sectors and those in other countries, are willing and able to buy in a time period. The book places emphasis on the importance of negative aggregate demand (AD) shocks, meaning decreases in aggregate demand. Chapter 3 illustrates the frequent inability of the natural logarithm of U.S. real GDP (or real output, the constant-buying-power-dollar value of final goods including services produced in the U.S.) to return to its pre-recession trend following the onsets of recessions, including negative-AD-shock recessions.

Starting with Chapter 5, this book presents results about the potential importance of aggregate demand from more formal hypothesis testing, particularly in light of concerns about conducting statistical inference using the very simple equations in Chapter 3. Much, though not all, of the evidence presented suggests that recessions are associated with breaks in the trend line for the natural log of real GDP. For the U.S. data, it appears that more than one break may be found in both the natural log of *total* U.S. real GDP and *per capita* U.S. real GDP. Therefore, I draw the conclusion that changes in population or changes in the population growth rate alone fail to explain all breaks in the U.S. real GDP series.

This book also presents evidence of possible downward breaks in the series for the natural log of U.S. nonfarm payroll employment. These possible breaks occur around recessions and could be associated with possible breaks in real output. Given that most of the breaks associated with recessions are downward breaks, with either a decrease in the intercept of the trend line or the slope of the trend line (or perhaps both), the failure of economies to return to their pre-recession trends has clear negative implications for living standards in the U.S. and other countries.

Perhaps it would in the vernacular qualify as a 'spoiler alert' at this point to state that this book focuses on the importance of aggregate demand. Many of the results to follow with data from the U.S. will stress the importance of aggregate demand. However, in light of the recent surge in inflation rates around the world, economists need to remember that aggregate supply factors are very important. In simple principles of macroeconomics terms, how can we determine the equilibrium price level without both the aggregate demand (AD) function and the aggregate supply (AS) function in the AD/AS or AS/AD diagram? More about the importance of aggregate supply will follow.

Before discussing results from the U.S. in detail and the importance of the results, let's first discuss mainstream macroeconomic views on recessions, particularly recessions caused by decreases in aggregate demand. For the purposes of this book and approaching the topic chronologically, the first major school of macroeconomic thought to be covered in this book is the classical school. A major tenet of the classical school of macroeconomic thought is that all prices (including wages, salaries, and interest rates) adjust rapidly following shocks or disturbances in the economy. Because of the assumption of price flexibility, the impact of aggregate demand shocks (and likely also the impact of *temporary* aggregate supply shocks) fades away quickly. In classical macroeconomic analysis, aggregate supply shocks and more specifically perhaps only permanent aggregate supply shocks have a lasting impact on long-run equilibrium real GDP, which would likely be synonymous with the terms potential real GDP and trend real GDP.

In turn, positive AD shocks (and perhaps also temporary AS shocks) do not cause a permanent change in potential real GDP or trend real GDP. Also, note that economists frequently or usually if not always assume that trend real GDP or potential real GDP increases over time, following an upward-sloping curve.

Classical macroeconomic analysis, at least in its most extreme form, views positive AD shocks and negative AD shocks symmetrically. Following an increase in aggregate demand, classical analysis emphasizes that prices in the economy increase rapidly. In the most extreme classical analysis, price levels jump instantaneously to new higher equilibrium levels following an increase in aggregate demand. Therefore, the most extreme classical analysis finds no increase in equilibrium real GDP after an increase in aggregate demand. Price levels simply rise instantly so that the various demanders in the economy (domestic households, domestic businesses, domestic government sectors, and those in other countries) have no ability to buy more goods and services produced in the domestic economy following an increase in aggregate demand in the most extreme classical analysis because higher price levels reduce the ability of demanders to buy goods and services, all other things equal.

In less extreme classical analysis, following an increase in aggregate demand, price levels rise quickly but not immediately to their new long-run equilibrium levels. Therefore, it is possible for increases in aggregate demand to lead to an increase in real GDP in the short term in the classical macroeconomic school of thought before price levels reach their new long-run equilibrium levels. But, in these less strict interpretations of classical macroeconomic analysis, real GDP decreases back to its long-run equilibrium level when all prices have had the opportunity to adjust fully to the greater level of demand in the economy. Further, although this does not happen immediately in less strict classicism, it happens rather quickly.

Decreases in aggregate demand have essentially the opposite results in classical macroeconomic analysis. Following a negative AD shock, in the most extreme version of the classical school, prices (including wages, salaries, and interest rates) fall instantaneously to their new lower long-run equilibrium levels. Despite the decrease in demand in the economy, the various demanders can afford to buy more goods and services at the new lower price level all other things equal. Thus, in the most extreme interpretation of the classical school of thought, real GDP does not decrease despite the decrease in aggregate demand. Less strict interpretations of classicism allow for short term (and likely *very* short term) decreases in real GDP due to a drop in demand before prices decrease fully to their new equilibrium levels. Again, the classical macroeconomic school of thought emphasized that prices would fall quickly following decreases in aggregate demand. Thus, an economy would soon be back at the long-run equilibrium real GDP (or the potential or trend real GDP) following a negative AD shock. In turn, the economy would not suffer a downward break in the trend curve or the trend line for real GDP.

The Great Depression may have been a 'game changer' in terms of macroeconomic theory. This part of the book that you are now reading will focus on two main challengers to classical macroeconomic theory, the Keynesian school and the monetarist school. Much of the time if not most of the time, readers can consider other schools of macroeconomic thought as sub-parts of either the classical, Keynesian, or monetarist schools.

Many countries experienced relatively long departures of production from their trends during the Great Depression era. In the U.S., it took about *ten years* for production to return to its level from either 1928 or

1929 before its plunge, according to data in Dornbusch et al. (2008, p. 462) attributed to *The National Income and Product Accounts of the United States, 1929–1974* from the U.S. Department of Commerce (n.d.). Readers should realize that returning to the level of production from before the Great Depression is not the same as returning to the *trend* of production from before the Great Depression. Due to factors such as technological improvements, trend production in an economy is often if not usually or always assumed to be increasing over time.

As an aside, the main measure of production years ago was real Gross National Product (GNP) rather than real Gross Domestic Product (GDP). Gross National Product measures the market value of goods and services produced by the citizens of a country within a quarter or a year despite whether they are living domestically or abroad. By contrast, Gross Domestic Product measures the market value of goods and services produced within national borders regardless of whether the producers are citizens of that country. Many economists use the terms GDP, GNP, and output synonymously at least at times. They also realize that the value of the goods and services produced as a part of output represents gross income generated from producing those goods and services.

Returning focus to the Great Depression, the part of macroeconomics that concentrates on measuring production of economies (meaning measuring output, GNP, and GDP), National Income Accounting, did not exist at least in any form similar to what it is today, until after the start of the Great Depression. In fact, if my understanding is correct, statistics for Gross National Product were not even calculated until after the onset of the Great Depression, with Simon Kuznets receiving credit for developing National Income Accounting. I do not recall Gross Domestic Product being calculated until either the very late 1980s or the early 1990s.

Output measures were not the only macroeconomic variables to suffer prolonged drops during the Great Depression. Unemployment rates surged in many countries as a result of the Great Depression and remained elevated for a while, implying a long drop in employment. Dornbusch et al. (2008, p. 462) report that with U.S. Bureau of Labor Statistics data (revised) in Darby (1976), the estimated unemployment rate in the U.S. measured on an annual basis rose to nearly 25%. I seem to recall either reading or hearing that at least some believe that on a monthly basis, the estimated unemployment rate in the U.S. may have reached about 33% in at least one month during the Great Depression.

If prices and other factors adjusted so rapidly to shocks, then why was output so low and why were unemployment rates so high for relatively long periods? The Keynesian and monetarist schools of thought set out to explain how economies could have experienced extended periods of unsatisfactory performance.

The first of those two schools of thought was the Keynesian school. The earliest generally acknowledged work in the Keynesian school was *The General Theory of Employment, Interest, and Money* by John Maynard Keynes (1964). Readers should realize that Keynes' (1964) landmark contribution was first published in 1936. I interpret Keynes (1964, for example pp. 210, 243–244, 257–279) to mean that in his view, classical macroeconomics tried to explain economic downturns with market imperfections such as rigidities. I further interpret Keynes (1964) to mean that classical macroeconomists (perhaps grudgingly) pointed to what they believed was a sluggishness of interest rates to fall sufficiently to return economies to growth. Their policy prescription was to use expansionary monetary policy to lower interest rates. In their model which at least implicitly had two periods, lower interest rates would stimulate more consumption in the earlier period (as opposed to a later period) and return economies to growth.

Rather than focusing on the behavior of consumers, Keynes (1964, Chapters 3, 5, and 6) placed more emphasis on the behavior of entrepreneurs. In his groundbreaking work, he reasoned that entrepreneurs would hire workers as long as they believed that hiring would be profitable. His analytical apparatus assumed that entrepreneurs had to believe that they would have sufficient demand from customers for the goods and services that the entrepreneurs would produce. Otherwise, it would not be profitable for them to continue hiring and employing labor.

In the model that Keynes set forth with aggregate supply and aggregate demand (somewhat different from modern textbook models of aggregate supply and aggregate demand), economies could and (likely) would remain at levels of employment short of all resources being fully employed. Although Keynes may have argued for both expansionary fiscal policy and expansionary monetary policy, many if not most early Keynesian economists focused on using expansionary fiscal policy to produce economic growth. Such measures include reductions in taxes and increases in government expenditures, the latter including both government purchases where a good or a service is produced in exchange for a payment from the government, and government transfer payments such as Social Security, where no good or service is produced in exchange.

Milton Friedman and the other economists conducting research in the monetarist school of macroeconomic thought offered a somewhat different (and some might say a very different) explanation for the subpar macroeconomic performance during the Great Depression. While Keynesian economists would likely list insufficient demand in the economy as one of the most important factors if not the single most important factor, on the other hand monetarism would point to a substantial decrease in the money supply as the most important factor.

Some point out that monetarists actually focus on changes in the inflation rate, meaning changes in the percentage change in the price level, as being the main driver of business cycle fluctuations. However, monetarists also find a high degree of correlation between the money supply in an economy and the price level in that economy. In turn, monetarism is often associated with the view that changes in the money supply growth rate are the main factor causing changes in the rate of inflation. Again in turn, changes in the rate of inflation are the main drivers of business cycle fluctuations in monetarism, but at least some point out that in monetarism, it is often if not usually changes in the money supply growth rate causing changes in the price level growth rate, also known as the rate of inflation.

Despite these differences between the monetarist school of macroeconomic thought and the Keynesian school of macroeconomic thought, both of these two schools of macroeconomic thought agree that prices and other factors do not necessarily adjust rapidly following shocks in the economy. If this is not clear in the case of *monetarist* analysis, then consider what happens following a change in the money supply in an economy. In *classical* analysis, an increase in the money supply results in a rapid increase in price levels, with the most extreme interpretation of classical analysis viewing the jump to the new long-run equilibrium price level instantaneously. The analysis is symmetric in classical analysis following a *decrease* in the money supply level. In classical analysis, the price level falls very soon to its new long-run equilibrium level, again with price levels reaching their new long-run equilibrium instantly in the most extreme classical interpretation. In the most extreme form of classical macroeconomics, changes in the money supply *cannot* cause a change in real GDP, even for a fleeting moment.

By relaxing the assumption that prices and other factors adjust to long-run equilibrium levels very rapidly, both the monetarist school and the Keynesian school of thought can explain changes in aggregate demand leading to changes in real GDP, at least in the short term. Readers should recall that changes in the money supply cause changes in aggregate demand in the short run. The thinking is that with more or fewer units of currency (i.e. U.S. dollars) circulating in an economy, the various demanders can afford to buy more or fewer goods and services produced (unless, of course, price levels rise or fall by the same percentage as the percentage increase in the money supply).

As presented in mainstream macroeconomics textbooks recently if not presently, the impacts of aggregate demand shocks fade away. This is true not only for the classical school but also for monetarism and modern mainstream Keynesianism. In turn, given time, economies will return to the natural rate of unemployment, presumably getting the maximum sustainable production given the resources and technology available. To clarify, at least some probably view the natural rate of unemployment as being interchangeable with 'full employment.'

1.2 Keynes' View on Full Employment in *The General Theory of Employment, Interest, and Money*

Keynes (1964, pp. 249–252) noted that full employment was not essentially guaranteed given sufficient time for people in an economy to adjust to shocks. In fact, he was concerned that it would be much more likely that forces existed in economies to prevent full employment in many and perhaps most situations.

Recently if not still presently, mainstream textbook analysis often focuses on rigidities in wages and other prices as the main reason why changes in aggregate demand would lead to changes in real GDP in the short run, when some prices are fixed due to contracts and other factors. Keynes (1964, p. 210) astutely pointed out that a decision not to spend a unit of currency today does not guarantee that the unit of currency not spent today will be spent tomorrow.

This issue is important because some studies such as Martin et al (2014) find that economies like the U.S. economy and the U.K. economy have real GDP series that fail to return to their pre-recession trends after the onsets of recessions. According to Martin et al (2014), the output gap after a recession meaning the difference between potential or trend real output and actual real output is not closed by real output surging back to its pre-recession trend. Rather, they find that many studies use filtered variables to calculate a lower estimate for the growth of potential or trend real output. Although these economies usually if not always have *levels* of output that exceed the levels from before the onsets of recessions, these economies frequently if not usually or always fail to return to the projected levels of real output implied by the continued growth of real output had the recessions not occurred. In such cases, in a sense, these economies do not fully recover from recessions. These failures to recover fully have devastating implications for the well-being of millions of people.

1.3 A Brief Overview of This Book

This book has seven chapters. In part, I decided on that number of chapters given that my favorite album by The Moody Blues is titled *Seventh Sojourn.*

This chapter has discussed schools of macroeconomic thought only briefly. Readers may benefit from further discussion. They may also benefit from a literature review of empirical work on how long shocks can have a negative impact on real output.

Chapter 2 offers more of a literature review than the current chapter. The first part of that literature review focuses on the major schools of macroeconomic thought. The second part discusses some of the empirical work on the importance and the duration of aggregate demand shocks.

This book uses data from the U.S. to see in Chapter 3 if the U.S. economy has returned to an extremely simple estimate of trend following recessions. Given econometric concerns with the modeling strategy in Chapter 3, many if not all of which are discussed in Chapter 4, this book uses somewhat more complex models and techniques in Chapter 5 to address whether permanent changes have occurred in U.S. real output. In so doing, Chapter 5 also uses more formal hypothesis testing than Chapter 3. Chapter 5 presents evidence that U.S. real output is best categorized as being either trend stationary *with at least one break* or a true unit root process.

Chapter 6 also seeks breaks in the series for U.S. nonfarm payroll employment. Downward breaks in U.S. employment could be a contributing factor or a cause of downward breaks in U.S. real GDP.

The final chapter, Chapter 7, extends the sample period for some of the econometric work in earlier chapters. It also provides observations on the importance of the results to guide future work.

Much though not all of the evidence in Chapters 3, 5, 6, and 7 suggests that negative AD shocks in the U.S. as well as negative AS shocks may have been associated with breaks in the trend growth path for U.S. real output. If further work supports these findings, then U.S. policymakers and people in the U.S. (and other countries) may want to think seriously and enthusiastically about using more expansionary policies following the start of another recession. To emphasize, an economy returning to the original *level* of real GDP from before a recession does *not* guarantee that it has return to its pre-recession *trend* which would be at a *higher* output level. More expansionary policies could increase the likelihood of returning real GDP and employment to their pre-recession trends.

References

Darby, M. (1976, February). Three-and-a-half million U.S. employees have been mislaid: Or an explanation of unemployment, 1934–1941. *Journal of Political Economy, 84*, 1–16.

Dornbusch, R., Fischer, S., & Startz, R. (2008). *Macroeconomics* (10th ed.). McGraw-Hill Irwin.

Keynes, J. M. (1964). *The general theory of employment, interest, and money*. Harcourt (original publication in 1936 by Macmillan).

Martin, R., Munyan, T., & Wilson, B. A. (2014). Potential output and recessions: Are we fooling ourselves? *IFDP Notes*, Board of Governors of the Federal Reserve System. November 12, 2014. https://www.federalreserve.gov/econresdata/notes/ifdp-notes/2014/potential-output-and-recessions-are-we-fooling-ourselves-20141112.html

U.S. Department of Commerce. (n.d.). *The national income and product accounts of the United States, 1929–1974*.

CHAPTER 2

Literature Review of Major Schools of Macroeconomic Thought and Empirical Work

Abstract This chapter provides additional discussion of schools of macroeconomic thought, adding the neoclassical school, the New Keynesian school, and the post Keynesian school of thought to the discussion. This book would probably be best considered as a work in the post Keynesian school. The chapter briefly discusses the equation of exchange. Following this preliminary material, this chapter discusses some econometric work related to the duration of negative shocks. One related topic is whether real GDP has a unit root or whether it is trend stationary with at least one break. Critical for the current book is whether decreases in aggregate demand either (1) cause downward breaks or show up as shocks in a unit root process whose impact never completely fades, or (2) have impacts that fade away fairly quickly.

Keywords Keynesian school of macroeconomic thought · Monetarist school of macroeconomic thought · Classical school of monetarist thought · Post Keynesian school of macroeconomic thought · Secular stagnation · Aggregate demand · Breaks in trend · Hysteresis · Equation of exchange · GDP

H. C. Hartman, *Bad Breaks in Real GDP and Employment*,
https://doi.org/10.1007/978-3-031-57769-7_2

2.1 A Brief Introduction

Much of this book focuses on whether real GDP returns to its pre-recession trend following recessions induced by decreases in aggregate demand. Readers less familiar with the major schools of macroeconomic thought and those less familiar with time series econometric analysis will likely want to read the remainder of this chapter. Readers already familiar with those topics and looking for results from hypothesis testing may decide to omit this chapter and pick up with Chapter 3 or to review quickly information in the current chapter as needed before starting Chapter 3.

What have some researchers found about the ability of economies, as Taylor Swift might say, to 'shake off' the growth-reducing effects of negative aggregate demand shocks in the longer term? Further, when using a method that projects or includes estimates of trend total real GDP and trend per capita real GDP beyond recessions, do the comparisons in this book of actual real GDP and per capita real GDP to their projected pre-recession trends (or perhaps their full-sample-period trends) find that these series come back to their trends after recessions? Let's answer the first question first.

2.2 Schools of Macroeconomic Thought

Before discussing econometric studies related to the possible persistence of negative shocks, particularly negative AD shocks, it may benefit readers to have a brief review of the major schools of macroeconomic thought for some context as to where the question of how long decreases in aggregate demand can reduce economic growth fits in macroeconomic analysis. In much if not most of this brief review, I will consider the neoclassical school of macroeconomic thought to be essentially the same as the classical school, and I will initially consider the new Keynesian school of macroeconomic thought to be essentially the same as the Keynesian school. The first part of the review of both the classical and Keynesian schools of thought below focuses on a treatment that is similar to, if not the same as, a modern textbook-style presentation of each of the schools of thought. That is followed by a somewhat more complete presentation (so that we will focus on simpler classical analysis followed by more complete classical analysis before turning to Keynesian analysis), which will in turn be followed by a brief discussion of monetarism. Afterward, I briefly discuss neoclassical, new Keynesian, and post Keynesian analysis.

For those not familiar, an important concept for parts of this discussion is the equation of exchange. A modern version of the equation of exchange notes that the money supply (or the stock of money) multiplied by the velocity of money, where velocity refers to the average number of times per period that a unit of currency like the U.S. dollar trades in a transaction that is part of GDP, equals the price level times real GDP. Algebraically, the equation of exchange states that $M*V = P*Y$, with M representing the money supply, V representing velocity, P representing the price level (for example, the implicit GDP deflator), and Y representing real GDP. Note that $P*Y$ equals nominal GDP, measured in currency with buying power in the period in which nominal GDP is measured. By contrast, real GDP is measured in constant-buying-power currency for more meaningful comparisons between periods that can have different prices and thus differences in purchasing power of money. Some of the schools of macroeconomic thought discussed below placed great emphasis on one of two interpretations of the quantity theory of money, also discussed below.

In the classical school of macroeconomic thought, deviations of actual real GDP away from long-run equilibrium real GDP are usually if not always very short term if such real output deviations occur. If an increase in aggregate demand occurs, then in classical analysis, prices (including interest rates and wages and salaries) increase rapidly in light of the higher demand in the economy. The most extreme interpretation of classical macroeconomic analysis (where the aggregate supply function is a vertical line *immediately*) has price levels instantly jumping up to their new long-run equilibrium levels following an increase in aggregate demand, so that no change in real GDP in the economy occurs if the economy was at the long-run equilibrium level of real GDP before the positive aggregate demand shock. In other words, in the most extreme form of classical analysis, despite the increase in aggregate demand, real GDP will not budge, not even for a nanosecond!

The analysis in the classical school of macroeconomic thought is symmetric for a decrease in aggregate demand, at least in its most extreme form. Again, in the most extreme version of classical analysis, prices would drop instantly to their new long-run equilibrium levels following a decrease in aggregate demand, so that if the economy were at the long-run equilibrium level of real GDP before the decrease in aggregate demand, then real GDP would not decrease following the decrease in demand. The decrease in price levels increases buying power despite the decrease in aggregate demand, so that real GDP would remain in long-run equilibrium despite a fall in demand in the economy. Thus, in the most extreme interpretation of classical analysis, a change in real GDP must have been caused by a shift in the aggregate supply function.

The policy prescription to return real GDP to its long-run equilibrium level following a decrease in aggregate demand in the classical school of macroeconomic thought, particularly in more extreme forms and in the most extreme form of classical analysis, is simply to do nothing. Prices will fall so quickly, and other factors will adjust so rapidly that the best policy response is simply to wait and the economy will return to long-run equilibrium very soon, thus leading to a *laissez-faire* policy recommendation. (For a succinct overview of the views of classical analysis on policy compared with Keynesian and monetarist analysis and 'modern consensus' (the latter of which this book does *not* perfectly fit), readers can view Table 17–1 in Krugman and Wells [2009, p. 485]).

Of course, not all classical analysis assumed that the aggregate supply function was *instantaneously* vertical. Keynes (1964, p. 257) observed that classical macroeconomic analysis found sticky prices, or more specifically rigid nominal wages, responsible for departures from long-run equilibrium. The following will help readers to understand more fully the complexity of classical analysis in its totality. Keynes (1964, pp. 257, 292–293) pointed out that the division in prior economic analysis (nowadays, microeconomics versus macroeconomics) was such that at a more micro level, prices depended on factors such as the elasticities of supply and demand but that at a more macro level, some classical analysis had the price level depending only on the money supply with the real output supply elasticity equaling zero, while in other more advanced classical analysis, presumably as long as the two sides of the equation of exchange are equal, all things regarding the equation of exchange could potentially occur, making the analysis murky.

To further complicate things, Keynes (1964, pp. 295–296) seemed to attribute to some classical analysis the view that aggregate supply is perfectly flat up to the full-employment level of real output and then vertical at that level of output. More specifically, Keynes stated that in the quantity theory of money, an increase in the money supply would increase employment proportionately until no unemployment exists, at which point the money supply and the price level increase proportionately. The classical school of thought interpreted the quantity theory of money as the view that the velocity of money was essentially constant in the short term.

According to Mankiw (2007, p. 328), David Hume in the 1700s wrote that increases in the money supply led to increases in real output in the short term before all prices increased. Similarly, Krugman and Wells (2009, pp. 470–471) pointed out that even prior to 1930, economic analysis realized that money was not neutral in the short term, meaning that increases in the money stock could increase real GDP in the short run; but classical macroeconomics emphasized the long term rather than the short term, the latter of which may have been trivial in the classical view.

But, if prices are sticky when pressure exists for prices to increase, then greater aggregate demand could possibly result in real GDP being above its long-run equilibrium level, which presumably is the maximum production that the economy can sustain year after year after year given its resources and technology, but the higher production level is very temporary in classical analysis. In classicism, rapid price increases take buying power away from households, businesses, government sectors, and those in other countries, so that the amount of domestically produced goods and services that these 'demanders' will be willing and able to buy at a higher price level will quickly return to the long-run equilibrium level, in the classical view. Despite the possibility of sticky prices, classical macroeconomic theory apparently did not find a useful role for stabilization policy, at least in the view of Krugman and Wells (2009, pp. 469–471, 484–486).

The Great Depression, where (1) annual real output in the U.S. according to at least some estimates (such as those from the U.S. Commerce Department as listed in Dornbusch et al. [2008, p. 462]) was below its 1929 level for roughly a decade, and (2) other countries experienced deep and protracted periods of depressed output; gave rise to the Keynesian and the monetarist schools of macroeconomic thought. As presented in conventional textbook analysis recently if not presently, the Keynesian school of macroeconomic thought assumes that prices and other factors do not necessarily adjust rapidly to ensure a quick return to full employment following changes in aggregate demand.

In perhaps the most extreme textbook-style interpretation of Keynesian and classical macroeconomic theory, Dornbusch et al. (2008, pp. 101, 110–111) depict the Keynesian AS function as a horizontal line and the classical AS function as a vertical line. With this type of Keynesian aggregate supply function, changes in aggregate demand affect the level of real output but not the price level. In turn, it may be easier to understand why Krugman and Wells (2009, p. 485) noted that Keynesian analysis found that expansionary fiscal policies could help to increase employment and real output during economic downturns. Increases in government expenditures and reductions in taxes, both of which would be thought to shift the aggregate demand function rightward, would result in higher real GDP and lower unemployment rates after a recession had occurred, but no increase in the price level if the aggregate supply function was horizontal.

As was the case with classical macroeconomic theory, Keynesian macroeconomic theory is much more complex than it appears in its most extreme form. At least some modern-era analysis that many would likely classify as either Keynesian or new Keynesian would view the short-run aggregate supply function as upward sloping but the long-run aggregate supply (LRAS) function as being vertical. Textbooks such as Krugman and Wells (2009, Chapter 12 and pp. 453–460) that show a downward-sloping short-run Phillips curve associated with an upward-sloping short-run aggregate supply function and a vertical long-run Phillips curve (LRPC) related to a vertical LRAS function offer analysis suggesting that in the absence of negative aggregate supply shocks, an increase in aggregate demand can increase real GDP and reduce unemployment rates in the short run, but at the cost of a higher inflation rate. In the long run, however, the impact of the increase in aggregate demand fades away if the LRPC and the LRAS functions are vertical, because in that case, the unemployment rate will automatically return to the natural rate of unemployment, and real GDP will return to the long-run-equilibrium real GDP.

For those less familiar, to restate it, readers may be wondering 'Where do I draw the line?' for the LRAS and LRPC functions? The vertical LRAS function intersects the horizontal axis in the aggregate supply-aggregate demand diagram at the long-run equilibrium level of real GDP, which equals trend real GDP or potential GDP in a specific period. The LRPC intersects the horizontal axis in the Phillips curve diagram at the natural rate of unemployment. When an economy has had the opportunity to adjust to all shocks, thereby reaching what the music group (and not necessarily the football team) (the) Eagles would call 'the long run,' the level of real GDP would be the long-run equilibrium real GDP, and the unemployment rate would be the natural rate of unemployment.

As an aside, in modern textbook-style analysis, a one-time increase in the money supply level would spark an increase in the price level, but not a permanent increase in the inflation rate, which is the percentage change in the price level. However, an increase in the money supply growth rate would, all other things equal, lead to an increase in the rate of inflation.

In comparing Keynesian (perhaps in a relatively modern form) and monetarist analysis in a footnote, Mishkin (2004, pp. 635–636), using upward-sloping aggregate supply functions for the short term but a vertical line for the long term when analyzing the result of repeated increases in the money supply (which would repeatedly increase aggregate demand), stated that the two schools of thought (Keynesian and monetarist) differed solely on how much longer real output remains above long-run equilibrium, with more time in the Keynesian school. To the extent that this modeling represents a modern interpretation of Keynesian macroeconomics, it shows that Keynesian analysis is more complicated than what is implied by a horizontal aggregate supply function (where presumably the impact of a change in aggregate demand would not need to fade away barring a change in aggregate supply).

Further, Keynes (1964, pp. 249–252) himself expressed at the very least considerable skepticism about the ability of economic forces to produce full employment most of the time. His interpretation of macroeconomic stability was that economic forces often resulted in an economy reaching an equilibrium at less than full employment and remaining there for a while, perhaps indefinitely. My understanding of Chapters 3, 5, and 6 in *The General Theory of Employment, Interest, and Money* by John Maynard Keynes (1964) is that from an economy-wide perspective, entrepreneurs continue to hire employees as long as the proceeds that they expect to receive from employing that number of workers is at least as large as the minimum amount of proceeds that firms would require to find that level of employment profit-increasing (or perhaps not profit-reducing). My interpretation is that Keynes did not believe that adjustments in prices (including wages and salaries), interest rates, or other factors could guarantee that an economy would be at full employment much of the time, let alone most of the time. If that is the case, then the impact of a decrease in aggregate demand could persist for a while, if not indefinitely.

In turn, a clear role for expansionary stabilization policy exists, although Keynesian analysis initially focused more on fiscal policy than on monetary policy. According to Mishkin (2004, Chapters 23 and 24 and pp. 586–587, 604, 607–608, 617), although Keynes stressed that the impact of expansionary monetary policy on real output occurred by lowering interest rates, in turn stimulating investment in physical capital; many Keynesian economists focused on fiscal policy, perhaps exclusively. A possible contributing factor was that at times in the 1930s and the 1940s, nominal interest rates were low, possibly approaching a liquidity trap. Modern textbook-style analysis (such as in Dornbusch et al. [2008, pp. 253, 261] and Krugman and Wells [2009, pp. 463–465, 474–476, 484–485]) notes that in a liquidity trap, expansionary fiscal policy is effective in stimulating real GDP, but expansionary monetary policy is not. Mishkin (2004, pp. 607–608, 636) and others have noted that in more modern times, Keynesian economists hold the view that increases in the money supply can increase real output and nominal output, with real output rising perhaps only in the short run.

As noted above, early in the Keynesian school of thought, economists focused on expansionary fiscal policy to increase real GDP growth during a recession. Reducing taxes and increasing government spending would both be expansionary fiscal policies. The thinking was to give income to households and businesses, likely under the assumption that they would spend a fraction of their new-found income. The additional spending by households and firms would create additional income in the economy, with people spending a fraction of this second wave of income. People would spend part of the additional income received, creating yet another wave of income, and so on.

The additional spending would help to return the economy back to getting the maximum sustainable production possible from its resources and its technology at a minimum faster than simply waiting, and that could assume (unlike Keynes [1964] himself) that the economy will return to its pre-recession trend without expansionary policy. From the most extreme classical perspective, where the price level would rise instantly to its new long-run equilibrium level due to greater demand from the expansionary policy, the result of expansionary policy has the disadvantage of inflation (the increase in the price level) without the benefit of a faster return to the long-run equilibrium real GDP level, from which a prior decrease in aggregate demand before the expansionary policy could not have caused even a momentary departure.

Over the years, Keynesian economic analysis placed more emphasis on expansionary monetary policies (increasing the money supply or the growth rate of the money supply, reducing interest rates) to stimulate economic growth due to recessions. Perhaps this was due to the contribution of the monetarist school of economic thought.

Like the Keynesian school of thought, the monetarist school of thought assumed that the price level does not necessarily adjust rapidly to its long-run equilibrium level following changes in aggregate demand. For example, according to Mankiw (2007, p. 409), Milton Friedman held the view in 1968 that it could take roughly two-to-five years for the effects of unexpected inflation in lowering unemployment rates to fade away. The thinking may have been something like this. An unexpected increase in the money supply increases aggregate demand. Inflation rises unexpectedly with a delay as the result of greater aggregate demand. Contracts that have wages and other prices agreed upon for a period slow the upward adjustment process of the price level to the greater aggregate demand while the contracts are in effect. Real GDP is higher and unemployment rates are lower until the price level reaches its new long-run equilibrium level. In the long-run equilibrium, real GDP is back to its long-run equilibrium level and the unemployment rate is back to the natural rate of unemployment when the price level has reached its new long-run equilibrium level. However, real GDP could be above potential and the unemployment rate could be below its natural rate for approximately two-to-five years while the adjustment process plays out.

However (unlike either the Keynesian school of thought or the classical school of thought), Burton and Lombra (2006, pp. 516–517) and others noted that the monetarist school of thought focused on increases and decreases in the money supply (or in the growth rate of the money supply) in nominal form as the main driver of business cycle fluctuations. It may be that monetarism focused on changes in the inflation rate as the cause of business cycle fluctuations. However, the monetarist school of thought found or assumed strong correlation between the money supply growth rate and the rate of inflation as noted by Baumol and Blinder (2012, p. 300) and Mishkin (2004, pp. 634–636), so that changes in the money supply growth rate were the main cause of business cycle fluctuations through their impact on inflation rates.

While the velocity of money was nearly constant most of the time in the short term in classical macroeconomic analysis as per Mishkin (2004, pp. 518–519), Burton and Lombra (2006, pp. 516–517) and Baumol and Blinder (2012, p. 298) pointed out that velocity was not constant but rather predictable in monetarist analysis. At least some have suggested that this view of velocity by the monetarists amounted to a reinterpretation of the quantity theory of money. Binder (2023) noted that Tavlas (2023) pointed out that economists at the University of Chicago in the 1920s and the 1930s, who at the very least helped give rise to monetarism if they were not monetarists, emphasized their view that without a long-term monetary policy rule, the velocity of money was very unstable. However, this is not an aspect often associated with monetarism today and is mentioned here for completeness.

Although monetarists preferred expansionary monetary policy over expansionary fiscal policy to increase real GDP during an economic downturn based on information in Krugman and Wells (2009, pp. 477, 485), they *may* have seen more merit than classical economists in expansionary fiscal policy during recessions. The view of monetarists that expansionary monetary policy could increase real output when an economy was suffering a downturn suggests that monetarists probably concluded that the real-output-reducing impact of a decrease in aggregate demand could last a while (but likely not permanently).

Neoclassical macroeconomic analysis, as it is used by Dornbusch et al. (2008) on pages 550–552 and by others, refers to later works that to a large degree qualify as classical works except that neoclassical macroeconomics assumes that people in the economy have rational expectations. If people have rational expectations, then people use the total amount of public information in its entirety when making decisions, and they do so in a logical, utility-maximizing manner. The conclusion of neoclassical analysis is that unexpected policy changes under some conditions may possibly increase employment and real output temporarily, but expected policy changes have no impact. Thus, neoclassical analysis seems consistent with a *laissez-faire* approach to policy.

By contrast, new Keynesian analysis as the term is used by Dornbusch et al. (2008) on pages 554–555 and by others, studies and incorporates into macroeconomic models reasons why prices (and perhaps other factors) may not adjust rapidly to long-run-equilibrium levels despite people having rational expectations. Thus, expansionary policies (including expected policy changes) could increase real output and employment.

In terms of analyzing decreases in aggregate demand, such decreases in aggregate demand have either a very short-term impact or no impact on real GDP or unemployment rates in neoclassical analysis. The impact of decreases in aggregate demand can last longer in new Keynesian analysis, although not permanently if the economy was initially in long-run equilibrium.

Post Keynesian analysis at the macroeconomic level differs from at least some conventional textbook presentations of the Keynesian macroeconomic school of thought. One difference is that in the post Keynesian school, price rigidities and other inconsistencies with market perfection are not necessarily the factors causing an economy to function at less than full employment. Some features of post Keynesian analysis include an emphasis on aggregate demand, a focus on fiscal policy to increase real GDP, and the view that hysteresis (in this context meaning path dependence of real GDP on its past values) exists in the real GDP series so that there is not one relevant long-run equilibrium real GDP. Readers can refer to Aboobaker et al. (2016) and Davidson (2015) for additional information about post Keynesian macroeconomics.

To the extent that post Keynesian analysis correctly analyzes the possible duration of the impact of decreases in aggregate demand on future real GDP growth, people looking at the situation through the lens of classical analysis and probably also the lenses of the neoclassical, monetarist, and new Keynesian schools of thought could be in for a very long wait indeed for real output to return to its pre-recession trend without further expansionary policy following a downturn. It turns out that this period could be even longer than the period between Chicago Cubs World Series titles. Could this drawn-out period have inspired Dan Fogelberg to write the line in 'Longer' about how long heavens have had stars?.

This is not merely an academic exercise. Think of the additional goods and services that could have been produced if real GDP in the U.S. would have returned to its pre-recession trend, and think of the additional jobs that could have been created, perhaps at higher income levels. Now, think of the losses that people have experienced in terms of fewer goods and services consumed and reduced pay and/or spells of unemployment and/or underemployment. Is it all in the name of waiting for markets to equilibrate?

2.3 Econometric Work Related to the Duration of Negative Aggregate Demand Shocks

Before empirical analysis on how long the impact of negative aggregate demand shocks can persist, let's briefly discuss some earlier work related to the topic. For additional information within this book about earlier work, refer to Chapters 1 and 3. For additional information beyond that, refer to the works referenced and works in turn referenced by the works cited here.

According to Dornbusch et al. (2008, pp. 566–567), a traditional view holds that real GDP fluctuates above and below a smooth (or relatively smooth), upward-sloping curve. Aggregate demand shocks in this orthodoxy were the main reason why the value of real GDP in the economy was usually either greater than or less than an estimated trend.

Over the years, researchers have developed challenges to this traditional view. Nelson and Plosser (1982), according to information in Dornbusch et al. (2008, pp. 552, 567–569), found support for the view that aggregate supply shocks dominated aggregate demand shocks in determining the real output data series because the series for real output is difference stationary. Hamilton (1994, p. 444) also noted that Nelson and Plosser (1982) found many time series variables to have unit roots, meaning that they are difference stationary. A difference stationary variable has future forecasted values over long time horizons that depend on all past values of the variable. This implies that the value of the variable today in undifferenced form can have a permanent impact on future values of that variable. Sir Paul McCartney, as in the song 'Coming Up,' might say that shocks to difference stationary variables will not fade away. If the variable is integrated of order one (meaning the variable is I(1)), then the *change* in that variable or the *first difference* of that variable is stationary so that eventually all shocks to the first difference of that variable fade away. (A variable that is I(1) has a unit root but the first difference of the variable is stationary, or I(0), not having a unit root.)

My interpretation of Hamilton (1994, pp. 438–441) suggests that a variable that is trend stationary and also increasing has predicted values that will eventually return to its upward-sloping trend, while a variable that is difference stationary does not have predicted values that will eventually return to a constant trend (including even the possibility of a trend that is a horizontal line) unless the variable is considered in first difference form or 'change in' form). Although both AD and AS shocks were found to impact real output, my reading of Dornbusch et al. (2008, pp. 552, 567–569) is that Nelson and Plosser (1982) (or the interpretation of Nelson and Plosser [1982] by Dornbusch et al. [2008]) at least implicitly ruled out the possibility that aggregate demand shocks could have a permanent impact on future values of real output. Apparently, in their analysis, only aggregate supply shocks could have permanent ramifications for real output and thus dominated aggregate demand shocks in real output, given their finding that real output was difference stationary.

By contrast, Pierre Perron (1989), according to information in Dornbusch et al. (2008, pp. 569–570) and in Hamilton (1994, pp. 449–450), found that real output was trend stationary, but with at least one break (in the post-World War II era). The inference drawn from the work of Perron (1989) by Dornbusch et al. (2008, pp. 569–570) was that usually, aggregate demand shocks had more of an impact than aggregate supply shocks in determining whether real output was either above trend or below trend but that occasional aggregate supply shocks could cause a permanent change in the estimated trend. As discussed in a later chapter, the EViews 10 User's Guide II (2017, pp. 610–614) noted that in a later paper, Perron (1997) found an intercept break in the annual series for U.S. real Gross National Product (GNP) in the year 1929. This seems to have coincided with a large decrease in aggregate demand associated with the stock market crash and the Great Depression. (As an aside, the EViews 10 User's Guide II (2017, p. 612) stated that Perron (1997) reported the break as occurring in 1928 rather than in 1929 because the method in that paper used the last period before the break to note the breaking period rather than the first period after the break to note the breaking period. An additional aside is that gross national product (GNP) measures the production of all citizens of a country regardless of where they reside while producing, while GDP measures production inside the borders of a country without regard to whether the goods and services produced within the nation are by citizens. Readers may recall that years ago, real GNP used to be the main measure of production or output rather than real GDP.)

The origins of the theoretical possibility of real output either having a unit root or being trend stationary with breaks may possibly have been posed no later than the year 1936, in Keynes' *The General Theory of Employment, Interest, and Money*. Keynes (1964, p. 210) discussed the possibility of saving and thus not consuming in the present leading to lower expected future consumption, less production of consumption goods in the present, and perhaps also less investment in physical capital. Given that Keynes (1964, p. 210) noted that because not consuming but rather saving in the current period does not come with a clear agreement to consume at some point in the future, the result represents 'a net diminution' (p. 210) in aggregate demand, possibly persisting in the future. Because consumption is such a large part of real GDP in the U.S. (and perhaps many other economies), this thinking appears to me to be consistent with (1) real output either exhibiting a unit root or having at least one break in an otherwise trend stationary process, where either way real output is not necessarily heading back to just one constant value or a time-invariant constant trend, and (2) changes in aggregate demand having persistent effects, including possible breaks in trend.

At least somewhat similar to the Perron (1989) study with real output being trend stationary with a break is a paper from Lam (1990). According to Hamilton (1994, pp. 450–451), Lam (1990) found breaks in trend in 1957, 1973, 1980, and possibly 1969 or 1970. Negative aggregate supply shocks are identified later in this book and its online appendix occurring around the times of these breaks in trend found by Lam (1990), and as listed by Hamilton (1994, pp. 450–451).

According to Eo and Morley (2022), Summers (2014, 2015) stressed the importance of insufficient aggregate demand as a cause for hysteresis. An associated topic is secular stagnation, where Hansen (1939) may have been the first work in secular stagnation. In secular stagnation, an excessive amount of funds saved (greater than the quantity of funds that the economy will use for the production and installation of new machines, the construction of new buildings, and the manufacturing of unsold inventory) slows down the economy. My sense is that Eo and Morley (2022) interpreted Summers (2014, 2015) to mean that either a liquidity trap where nominal interest rates cannot fall any lower, perhaps being constrained by zero, or something close to a liquidity trap stopped the process where the quantity of funds 'supplied' by saving would decrease by having interest rates fall and where the quantity of funds 'demanded' by firms borrowing (to spend on investing in physical capital such as producing new buildings, machines, and inventories) would increase, again as interest rates would fall. This 'glut' of savings not spent winds up causing aggregate demand and real GDP to fall. The description of Summers (2014, 2015) and Hansen (1939) by Eo and Morley (2022) seems reasonable.

Eo and Morley (2022) point out that Blanchard et al. (2015) find that recessions in more than twenty countries have reduced the level and growth rate of real output. However, Blanchard et al (2015) note that aggregate supply factors could share some of the responsibility, at least as per Eo and Morley (2022), with the aggregate supply factors perhaps being solely responsible for the reduction in trend growth. Cerra and Saxena (2017), at least in the view of Eo and Morley (2022), question the usefulness of the theoretical concept of an output gap, given that Cerra and Saxena (2017) stress the permanent loss of output associated with recessions. That probably includes recessions due to decreases in aggregate demand.

Eo and Morley (2022) point out that Gordon (2015, 2016b) offers a different explanation of the growth slowdown in the U.S. Gordon (2015, 2016b) relies on changing demographics and a reduction in the growth of productivity, according to Eo and Morley (2022), to explain the less satisfactory economic performance. Again, Eo and Morley's (2022) summary of Gordon (2015, 2016b) seems reasonable. Among the supply-oriented factors listed by Gordon (2015, 2016a, 2016b) is the observation that starting around 1970, technological innovations have not been as broadly implemented as they were from about 1870 to 1970. While Gordon (2015, 2016b) noted that aggregate demand factors could also play a role, Summers (2014, 2015) acknowledged that aggregate supply factors could also be important.

Given that some have used Markov switching processes as an econometric modeling technique when using economic variables that apparently have at least one break, let's briefly discuss such models here. The Lam (1990) study uses a Markov switching process as per Hamilton (1994, pp. 450–451). Chapter 22 of Hamilton (1994) discusses switching processes including Markov switching processes. The basic idea behind a switching process is that more than one state or regime in the economy exists, and switching processes allow for the estimation of parameters in the model so that some of the parameters can vary between the regimes or states, but other parameters are invariant to the regime or the state. When used in a macroeconomic setting, the Markov switching technique estimates probabilities of the macroeconomy in one period being in one of at least two states and then in the immediately following period either remaining in the same state or switching into another state. Hamilton

(1994, p. 678) points out that the set of probabilities of being in a particular state in one period based on all of the past states is called a Markov chain.

In the view of Hamilton (1994, p. 677), econometricians should incorporate the chance of a change in the state meaning the likelihood of a change in the regime into forecasts when such probabilities exist. Further, frequently if not usually or always, the state change or regime change according to Hamilton (1994, p. 677) is a random variable. Hamilton (1994, p. 677) states that for completeness, the probabilities of changing between states should be estimated and incorporated into econometric models.

Eo and Morley (2022) is another example of a study using a Markov switching process. Readers can refer to Hamilton (1994, Chapter 22) and Eo and Morley (2022) for more references on Markov switching processes than included here. Eo and Morley (2022) estimate a model with states for two different types of recessions, one in which a recession is associated with a permanent loss of real GDP, and another in which a recession is not associated with a permanent reduction of real GDP. The third state of three has the economy expanding. Eo and Morley (2022) at least imply that their model is a Markov switching model for real GDP with random regimes where their model is perhaps more similar to some other studies rather than the approach of Huang et al. (2016) who assign NBER dates to recessions rather than having random regimes and may decide before econometric modeling whether a recession is L-shaped or U-shaped.

My sense is that of the schools of macroeconomic thought discussed above, the Nelson and Plosser (1982) study at least as it was presented in Dornbusch et al. (2008, pp. 552, 567–569) would be best categorized as either within the classical school or the neoclassical school, although not in their most extreme forms. If in that paper aggregate demand shocks can have a transitory impact on real GDP, then that would preclude the Nelson and Plosser (1982) study from being consistent with the most extreme form of classical analysis, where all changes in real GDP are at least implicitly due to changes in aggregate supply. However, the dominance of aggregate supply shocks would lead me to categorize the paper or at least its interpretation as classical or neoclassical.

Moreover, Dornbusch et al. (2008, pp. 552, 571) wrote that the Nelson and Plosser (1982) paper led to work on real business cycle (RBC) theory, which assumed speedy adjustments to changes in aggregate demand in the economy, and that RBC theory was an extension of the view that people use all public information in a logical way when making economic decisions. The latter feature that is at least implicitly part of RBC theory, known as rational expectations, in the previous sentence when combined with rapid price adjustments would place RBC theory in the category of neoclassical analysis. (If the Nelson and Plosser [1982] paper was an econometric study, then it may be difficult to categorize as in the classical or neoclassical school, or another school of macroeconomic thought. However, the interpretation of it by Dornbusch et al. [2008, pp. 552, 567–569] would reflect either classical or neoclassical analysis.)

As an econometric article, the Perron (1989) study may be more difficult to categorize. While the interpretation of Perron's (1989) paper by Dornbusch et al. (2008, pp. 569–570) finds that aggregate demand shocks do not necessarily have a permanent impact in Perron's (1989) study, their importance in determining business cycle fluctuations around a non-constant trend suggests in my view that Perron's (1989) paper could potentially be a Keynesian study, a new Keynesian study (where prices may not rapidly reach long-run-equilibrium levels despite people having rational expectations), or a monetarist study. The Keynesian influence is especially strong (1) if prices do not rapidly adjust to their long-run equilibrium levels in the Perron (1989) paper so that departures of real GDP away from its trend can last years and (2) if it is possible for a study to be Keynesian without having the impact of any aggregate demand shocks (including negative AD shocks) being truly permanent. The later study by Perron (1997) has at least one finding that could possibly be consistent with the post Keynesian school of thought, given that a negative shock in 1929 was associated with a downward break in U.S. real output. Given that the Perron (1989, 1997) studies may be econometric studies, it may be better to think about these studies as having findings consistent with one or more schools of macroeconomic thought rather than working directly in any of those schools.

Of the studies discussed in the most detail here in this book, the Eo and Morley (2022) study may possibly be the most difficult to categorize within one of the major schools of macroeconomic thought. While the finding that the Great Recession in the U.S. did not have an essentially permanent impact on U.S. real GDP would not support the post Keynesian view, the finding that the U.S. recessions of 1990–1991 and 2001 had permanent negative effects on U.S. real GDP could easily support that view, given decreases in inflation rates around those times of declining real output.

In my view, most if not all of the following studies in this paragraph have findings better classified as either Keynesian (including the new Keynesian and post Keynesian schools) or monetarist rather than as classical (or neoclassical). Again, it may be better to categorize the findings of these works rather than to assume that these studies or their authors adhere strictly to a particular school of macroeconomic thought. Among the findings of Cerra and Saxena (2008) was that in many if not all of the countries in their study, some of which may be developing, financial crises can lead to real GDP being lower than it would have been otherwise for several years, if not permanently, after a crisis occurs. Of course, financial crises all other things equal result in decreases in aggregate demand. Martin et al. (2014) use data from many countries, including the U.S., and find that negative aggregate demand shocks may possibly reduce economic growth permanently. Hartman (2013) suggested that decreases in aggregate demand could have a long-lasting impact on real GDP (at least indirectly by causing aggregate supply to shift) but had much less formal statistical analysis than either Martin et al. (2014) or Cerra and Saxena (2008). One of the goals of the book that you are now reading is to apply a more rigorous statistical examination than in Hartman (2013) to U.S. data.

References

Aboobaker, A., Köhler, K., Prante, F., & Tarne, R. (2016, December 18). *Post-Keynesian economics*. Accessed online May 21, 2019 at www.exploring-economics.org/en/orientation/post-keynesian-economics/

Baumol, W. J., & Blinder, A. S. (2012). *Macroeconomics: Principles and policy* (12th ed.). Southwestern Cengage Learning.

Binder, C. (2023). Book review of *The Monetarists: The making of the Chicago Tradition, 1927–1960* (By Tavlas, G. S. [2023]. *Journal of Economic Literature*, forthcoming).

Blanchard, O., Cerutti, E., & Summers, L. H. (2015). *Inflation and activity: Two explorations and their monetary policy implications* (IMF working paper, 15/230).

Burton, M., & Lombra, R. (2006). *The financial system and the economy: Principles of money and banking* (4th ed.). Thomson South-Western.

Cerra, V., & Saxenna, S. C. (2008). Growth dynamics: The myth of economic recovery. *American Economic Review, 98*(1), 439–457.

Cerra, V., & Saxena, S. C. (2017). *Booms, crises, and recoveries: A new paradigm of the business cycle and its policy implications* (IMF working paper, 17/250).

Davidson, P. (2015). *Post Keynesian theory and policy: A realistic analysis of the market oriented capitalist economy*. Edward Elgar.

Dornbusch, R., Fischer, S., & Startz, R. (2008). *Macroeconomics* (10th ed.). McGraw-Hill Irwin.

Eo, Y., & Morley, J. (2022). Why has the U.S. economy stagnated since the great recession? *The Review of Economics and Statistics, 104*(2), 246–258. https://doi.org/10.1162/rest_a_00957, accessed online at https://direct.mit.edu/rest/article/104/2/246/97713/Why-Has-the-U-S-Economy-Stagnated-since-the-Great

EViews 10 User's Guide II. (2017). IHS Global, Inc. Irvine, CA.

Gordon, R. J. (2015). Secular stagnation: A supply-side view. *American Economic Review, 105*(5), 54–59. https://doi.org/10.1257/aer.p20151102

Gordon, R. J. (2016a). Perspectives on *The Rise and Fall of American Growth*. *American Economic Review: Papers and Proceedings, 106*(5), 72–76.

Gordon, R. J. (2016b). *The rise and fall of American growth: The U.S. standard of living since the civil war*. Princeton University Press.

Hamilton, J. D. (1994). *Time series analysis*. Princeton University Press.

Hansen, A. (1939). Economic progress and declining population. *American Economics Review, 29*(1), 1–15.

Hartman, H. C. (2013). Where do we go from here? Considering policy options to complete the recovery from the great recession. *Journal of International Business Management and Research, 4*(13), 15–27.

Huang, Y., Luo, S., & Startz, R. (2016). *Are recoveries all the same: GDP and TFP?* (SSRN working paper 2988263).

Keynes, J. M. (1964). *The general theory of employment, interest, and money*. Harcourt (originally published in 1936 by Macmillan).

Krugman, P., & Wells, R. (2009). *Macroeconomics* (2nd ed.). Worth Publishers.

Lam, P. (1990). The Hamilton model with a general autoregressive component: Estimation and comparison with other models of economic time series. *Journal of Monetary Economics, 26*, 409–432.

Mankiw, N. G. (2007). *Brief principles of macroeconomics* (4th ed.). Thomson South-Western.

Martin, R. F., Munyan, T., & Wilson, B. A. (2014, November 12). *Potential output and recessions: Are we fooling ourselves?* (IFDP Notes). Washington: Board of Governors of the Federal Reserve System. https://doi.org/10.17016/2573-2129.06. http://www.federalreserve.gov/econresdata/notes/ifdp-notes/2014/potential-output-and-recessions-are-we-fooling-ourselves-20141112.html

Mishkin, F. S. (2004). *The economics of money, banking, and financial markets* (7th ed.). Pearson Addison Wesley.

Nelson, C. R., & Plosser, C. I. (1982). Trends and random walks in macroeconomic time series: Some evidence and implications. *Journal of Monetary Economics, 10*(2), 139–162.

Perron, P. (1989). The great crash, the oil price shock, and the unit root hypothesis. *Econometrica, 57*, 1361–1401.

Perron, P. (1997). Further evidence on breaking trend functions in macroeconomic variables. *Journal of Econometrics, 80*, 355–385.

Summers, L. H. (2014). US economic prospects: Secular stagnation, hysteresis, and the zero lower bound. *Business Economics, 49*(2), 65–73. https://doi.org/10.1057/be.2014.13

Summers, L. H. (2015). Demand side secular stagnation. *American Economic Review: Papers and Proceedings, 105*(5), 60–65.

Tavlas, G. S. (2023). *The monetarists: The making of the Chicago tradition, 1927–1960*. University of Chicago Press.

CHAPTER 3

Results from Estimating and Projecting Trends for Recent Recessions

Abstract Seeking evidence on the duration of aggregate demand shocks, this chapter estimates trends for the natural logs of total U.S. real GDP and per capita U.S. real GDP. This chapter uses simplistic estimates of trend, with only (a) an intercept or a constant, (b) a time trend multiplied by a coefficient, and (c) an error term or a residual as the only variables on the right side of the regression equation, with somewhat more complex regression equations that are sensitive to standard regression assumptions in later chapters. Trend equation estimates differ based on the starting and ending quarters. The body of this chapter has results focusing mainly on whether U.S. total real GDP and U.S. per capita real GDP returned to pre-recession trends after the dot-com-bubble recession and the Great Recession. Most of the discussion of other recessions appears in the online-only appendix. Using this simplistic estimate of trend, U.S. total real GDP and U.S. per capita real GDP often though not always failed to return to pre-recession trends after the onsets of recessions regardless of whether the recessions were caused by aggregate demand shocks or aggregate supply shocks.

Keywords Breaks in real GDP trend · Aggregate demand · Aggregate supply · Recessions · Expansions · Business cycles · Trend · Great Recession · Dot-com-bubble recession · Output gap

H. C. Hartman, *Bad Breaks in Real GDP and Employment*,
https://doi.org/10.1007/978-3-031-57769-7_3

3.1 Introductory Comments

Let's get ready to look at the empirical evidence of whether the U.S. economy completely recovered from past recessions, including the Great Recession. For the purpose of this book, given that the economy usually grows over time, *fully completing* a recovery from a recession requires not only that real GDP returns to the level of real GDP before the recession, but it also requires that real GDP fully returns to the trend around which the economy had been fluctuating before the recession. In other words, I will assume that the economy has not fully recovered from a recession until the level of real output in at least one quarter after a recession is at least as large as the level implied by projecting the pre-recession trajectory forward.

My guess is that most readers would probably be most interested in the results for the Great Recession because it is as of this writing the most recent U.S. recession that has several years of data for its post-recession recovery and also by many measures (if not most or all) one of the most severe recessions since the Great Depression, with only the COVID-19-associated recession being much deeper but much shorter. Therefore, I present results from the Great Recession first. Similarly, because readers may have more interest in more recent recessions than recessions that started in the 1940s or the 1950s, I will discuss recessions in reverse chronological order, or most recent first, and most of the discussion of the results from recessions before the dot-com-bubble recession will be only in the online appendix.

The total U.S. real GDP data in this chapter were accessed from www.economagic.com on November 2, 2016 (but may have been obtained through the Saint Louis Federal Reserve) and were likely compiled by the U.S. Bureau of Economic Analysis. Also accessed on November 2, 2016, the per capita U.S. real GDP data were compiled by the U.S. Bureau of Economic Analysis (2016) and were found on the Saint Louis Federal Reserve FRED web page. Much of the econometric work in this chapter and in Chapters 4 and 5 will have the second quarter of 2016 as the last quarter within the sample period, although the estimation of trends in the current chapter will often end before the second quarter of 2016. Some of the econometric analysis will be extended through the fourth quarter of 2019 in Chapter 7. The results will be fairly similar if not very similar.

To be further discussed near the end of this chapter, one table summarizes whether or not the natural logs of total U.S. real GDP and per capita U.S. real GDP returned to exceeding or at least reaching their pre-recession trends after dropping below around the onsets of recessions as identified in this chapter and its online appendix. The table lists the recessions in the usual chronological order (from earliest to most recent). Also to be further discussed near the end of the chapter, another table offers approximations of the constant term and the time trend for regression equations estimated for the Great Recession and the dot-com-bubble recession, with more in the online appendix.

3.2 The Great Recession

In examining results from the Great Recession, first consider Fig. 3.1. This figure shows the natural log of quarterly real GDP (LNY) in billions of 2009-buying-power U.S. dollars and at a seasonally adjusted, annualized rate from the first quarter of 1947 through the second quarter of 2016, which is the full sample period for this chapter. Figure 3.1 also shows the trend for the natural log of real GDP (TREND_LNY_FULLSMPL) over the same period estimated using data from the first quarter of 1947 through the second quarter of 2016. The data are in natural log form to make them either more linear (in the case of LNY) or perfectly linear (in the case of TREND_LNY_ FULLSMPL).

Obviously, the series for the natural log of real GDP oscillates to some degree around the estimated trend in Fig. 3.1. However, notice near the right part of Fig. 3.1, the natural log of real GDP fell below the estimated trend with the onset of the Great Recession in the first quarter of 2008. Just one quarter earlier, in the fourth quarter of 2007, the series was still slightly above TREND_LNY_FULLSMPL. But, LNY fell below the estimated trend in the Great Recession and had not returned to the estimated trend by the second quarter of 2016. The apparent failure of U.S. real GDP to return to trend following the Great Recession is one of the main themes of this book. The frequent failure of US real GDP to come back to pre-recession trends reminds me of the announcer in the opening theme song and credits for some seasons of the TV sitcom version of 'The Odd Couple' starring Jack Klugman and Tony Randall saying, 'never return....'

With the focus on real output being unable to return to pre-recession trends in many cases following a recession, most of the graphs to follow in

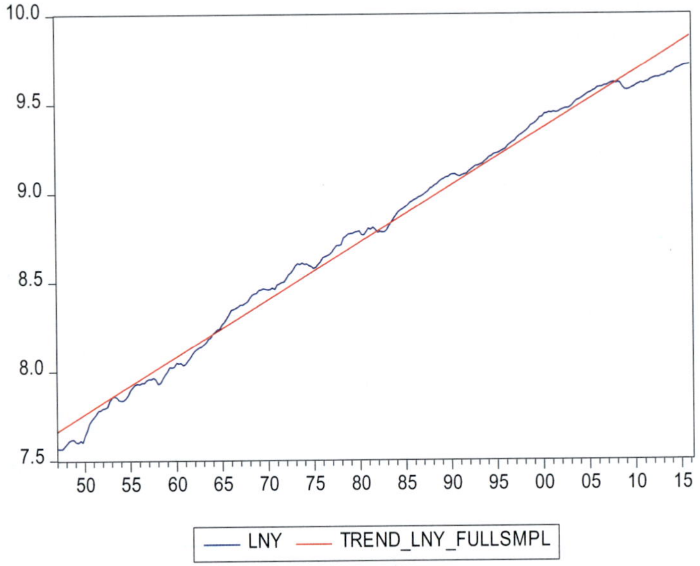

Fig. 3.1 Quarterly data for the natural log of U.S. real GDP, annualized and seasonally adjusted, and the trend of the natural log of U.S. real GDP from the first quarter of 1947 through the second quarter of 2016 (*Sources* www.economagic.com, U.S. Bureau of Economic Analysis, Saint Louis Federal Reserve Bank, and the author's calculations)

this chapter will show variables that compare the natural log of actual U.S. real GDP in total or in per capita form with an estimate of the trend of the log of real GDP, again, either in total or per capita. More specifically, these variables that I refer to as 'gap variables' subtract an estimate of the trend growth path for the natural log of total or per capita real GDP in a quarter from the actual natural log of either total or per capita real GDP in the same quarter. Clearly, a positive value for a gap variable in a quarter means that real GDP is greater than its estimated trend in that quarter, while a negative value for a gap variable indicates that real GDP is below the estimated trend.

Figure 3.2 can help readers to visualize the relationship between the variables. The top set of axes with real output data in natural log form reproduces what is shown in Fig. 3.1 for ease of comparison with the gap variable in the second set of axes in Fig. 3.2.

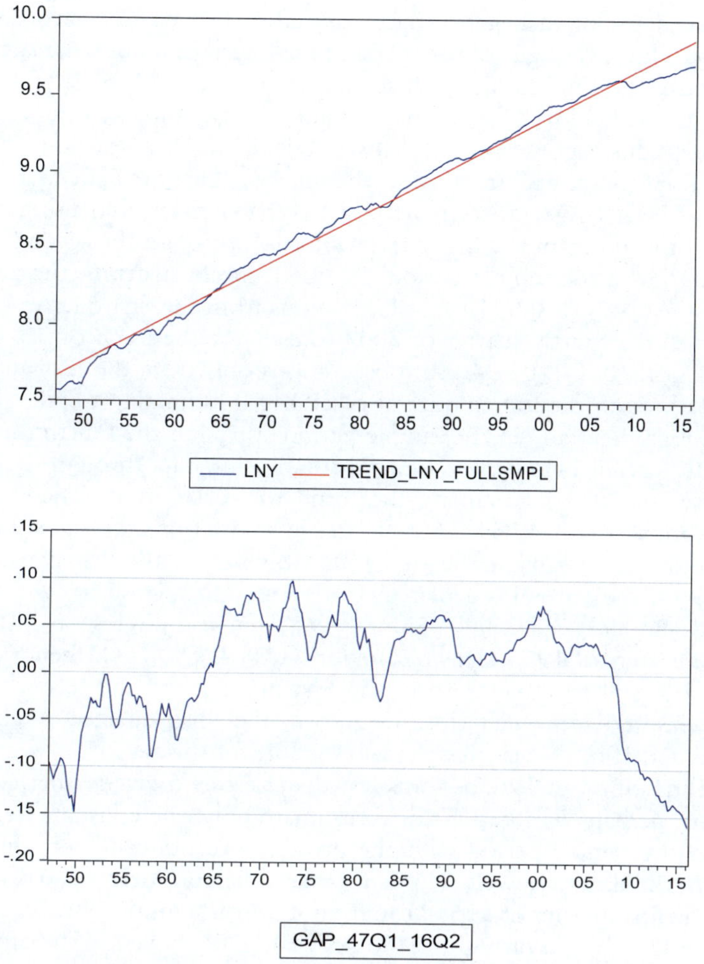

Fig. 3.2 Relationship between U.S. real GDP in natural log form, its estimated trend (both in the top set of axes) and the estimated gap variable with the trend estimated from the first quarter of 1947 through the second quarter of 2016 (*Sources* www.economagic.com, U.S. Bureau of Economic Analysis, Saint Louis Federal Reserve Bank, and the author's calculations)

The name of each gap variable has after the first underscore symbol ('_') the last two digits of the year and the quarter number, the latter after the letter 'Q,' indicating the first quarter of data used to estimate trend. After the second underscore in the name of a gap variable, the second set of two digits represents the last two digits of the last year in which data were used to estimate trend, with the quarter duly noted afterward. Thus, GAP_47Q1_16Q2 represents the gap variable calculated using an estimate of trend from the first quarter of 1947 through the second quarter of 2016, the full sample period. Similarly, in constructing the gap variable, GAP_47Q1_07Q4 uses observations from the first quarter of 1947 through the fourth quarter of 2007 to estimate the trend of real output, while GAP_01Q1_07Q4 uses observations only from the first quarter of 2001 through the fourth quarter of 2007 for estimating trend.

Notice that early in the sample period (through the fourth quarter of 1963), LNY is below the estimated trend using data through the second quarter of 2016 to estimate the trend for real output. Therefore, the gap variable GAP_47Q1_16Q2 in the second set of axes is less than zero through the fourth quarter of 1963. However, in the first two quarters of 1953, the natural log of real GDP was rather close to its estimated trend and close again in 1955 and 1963 but not as close as in the first two quarters of 1953. This resulted in GAP_47Q1_16Q2 being close to zero but still less than zero in the first quarter and the second quarter of 1953 and somewhat close to zero in the third quarters of the years 1955 and 1963. Given that the gap variable for this seventeen-year period (1947q1 through 1963q4) was less than zero and given other considerations, perhaps it is better not to estimate only one constant trend over a lengthy sample period with the possible exception of only one trend fitting the data very well. This is a topic to be considered shortly.

The first quarter of 1964 brought not only the musical British Invasion to the U.S. It also brought the log of real GDP above its estimated trend for the first time in the sample period. LNY then remained above the estimated trend through the fourth quarter of 1981, a span of eighteen years. LNY was less than TREND_LNY_FULLSMPL from the first quarter of 1982 through the second quarter of 1983, resulting in negative values for GAP_47Q1_16Q2 during those quarters, as shown in Fig. 3.2.

From the third quarter of 1983 through the fourth quarter of 2007, the actual natural log of U.S. real GDP exceeded its trend, producing positive values for the gap variable. The first quarter of 2008 brought not only the Great Recession to the U.S. based on quarterly data but also the return to negative values for the gap variable which continued through the second quarter of 2016 (and probably substantially beyond).

At least some may be interested in approximately how far real GDP was percentagewise either above or below its estimated trend in a particular quarter. The good news is that it is relatively simple to obtain an estimate due to the properties of natural log differences. For small differences (for example, a small difference between the actual natural log of real GDP and its estimated trend), the natural log difference is roughly equal to the percentage difference (for instance, the percentage difference between the natural log of real GDP and its trend) divided by 100.

To give an example, consider the value of the gap variable in the third quarter of 2008. This was the third consecutive quarter of GAP_47Q1_16Q2 being less than zero. The gap variable took on a value of approximately −0.0223 during the third quarter of 2008. Using actual real GDP and its trend both in levels and not in natural log form, I calculate that actual real GDP in the third quarter of 2008 was approximately 2.20% below the trend estimated over the sample period through the second quarter of 2016. Therefore, given that the gap variable value for that quarter shows that the natural log difference was about 0.0223, multiplying that by 100 gives roughly 2.23%, just a bit more than the approximately 2.20% actual gap. Note that in some cases to follow where the natural log differences may be comparatively large, I may report the percentage difference between a measure of real GDP (total or per capita) and its trend, *neither* in natural log form. In other cases, I may simply multiply the log difference by 100. I may also report both the actual percentage difference and the gap variable approximation, the latter multiplied by 100.

The correspondence between the natural log difference multiplied by 100 and the percentage difference diverges as the percentage differences grow larger, although the natural log difference (multiplied by 100) may still give a useful, very rough estimate. Considering the last quarter in the diagram, the second quarter of 2016, the gap variable was roughly −0.163, or about a 16.3% difference based on the gap variable method. On the other hand, when using the actual level of real GDP and the actual trend of real GDP, neither in natural log form, I calculate that during the second quarter of 2016, actual real GDP was approximately 15.0% below the trend estimated from data from the first quarter of 1947 through the second quarter of 2016. Thus, the natural log difference (times 100) is not as close to an estimate of the percentage difference between actual real GDP and trend when the natural log difference is not relatively small.

Regardless of whether 15.0% or 16.3% better represents how far real GDP was below trend, this represents a large shortfall of real GDP below its trend. Imagine all of the additional goods and services that we could produce in the U.S. if the economy were producing between fourteen and seventeen percent more each year! Think about all of the additional needs and wants that could be satisfied but are unfortunately not being satisfied.

Because the U.S. economy has not returned to its trend following the Great Recession, the economy did not fully recover from the Great Recession during the Not-So-Great Recovery, (at least in terms of the way that the book that you are now reading would consider a complete economic recovery). However, using all of the data from the first quarter of 1947 through the second quarter of 2016 to estimate the trend may not be the best way to estimate the trend. As others have noted, recessions could potentially be associated with breaks in the trend. Keeping that in mind, let's look at results using data from the first quarter of 1947 through the fourth quarter of 2007, the last quarter before the beginning of the Great Recession, to estimate the trend. Afterward, we will look at results estimating the trend using data from the beginning of the previous recession, the first quarter of 2001, through the fourth quarter of 2007. We will also consider results obtained using per capita real GDP rather than real GDP in total.

When estimating the trend for the natural log of real GDP using data from the first quarter of 1947 through the fourth quarter of 2007, real GDP was last above trend in the fourth quarter of 2000. In that quarter, real GDP was about one percent above trend. By the fourth quarter of 2007, real GDP was about six percent below its trend, not having returned to trend after the beginning of the dot-com-bubble recession prior to the start of the Great Recession. However, the gap variable continued to grow more negative most quarters after the fourth quarter of 2007, reaching about −0.24 in the second quarter of 2016, and amounting to real GDP being about 22% below its estimated trend in that quarter.

In fact, GAP_47Q1_07Q4 was further below zero than GAP_47Q1_16Q2 in the second quarter of 2016 by roughly 0.08, implying that actual real GDP was more than 6.5% further below its trend estimated when using data from the first quarter of 1947 through the fourth quarter of 2007 to estimate the trend than actual real GDP was below trend from data from the first quarter of 1947 through the second quarter of 2016. The inclusion of the Great Recession and the Not-So-Great Recovery in the estimation of trend caused a notable reduction in the trend, particularly by the end of the sample period.

Because recessions could possibly cause breaks in trend or otherwise alter the estimation of trend, we will also consider the comparison of the actual natural log of real GDP to an estimated trend using data only from the first quarter of 2001, the first quarter of the dot-com-bubble recession, through the fourth quarter of 2007, the last quarter of expansion before the Great Recession. Note that a failure to include *any* quarters of recession in the estimation of trend could give excessive estimates of trend growth. I will not analyze trends that do not include episodes that qualify as recessions as defined in this book despite the fact that recessions could potentially cause breaks in trend because (1) it may be unrealistic to estimate a trend with either no quarters of contraction or only an occasional contractionary quarter, and (2) if the estimation of pre-recession trend includes quarters of contraction but recessions are followed by a failure of real GDP to return to its pre-recession trend (including data from the previous recession) after the economy starts growing again, then any estimations of pre-recession trend around those times that either nearly eliminate or completely eliminate episodes of contraction from the estimation of trend (which would probably find even higher estimates of trend growth) would likely also imply a failure to return to trend.

Table 3.1 lists the durations of recessions (as identified in the book that you are now reading) from the first quarter of 1947 through the second quarter of 2016. Loosely speaking, in this book recessions are mainly if not exclusively periods with at least two quarters of decreasing total real GDP where the quarters are either consecutive or relatively close, thus possibly indicating a break in the trend growth path of the log of real GDP. Although many may consider the periods of decreasing output in the early 1980s in the U.S. as two separate recessions, this study considers them as part of one recession, especially because it makes little sense in my opinion to think that the U.S. economy first established a new clear trend as real GDP started falling in the second and third quarters of 1980 (based on data from www.economagic.com) and then established yet another new clear trend so soon afterward when real output decreased in the second and fourth quarters of 1981 and the first and third quarters of 1982, with the second quarter of 1981 only three quarters after the third quarter of 1980.

When estimating trend with data from the first quarter of 2001 through the fourth quarter of 2007, the natural log of real GDP last exceeded its trend in the fourth quarter of 2006. In each quarter of 2007, the natural log of real GDP was just below its trend, with the greatest shortfall of the log of real output below trend in the year 2007 occurring in the fourth quarter of 2007 with a value of approximately −0.0087. This implies that real GDP was roughly 0.87% below its estimated trend in the fourth quarter of 2007, obviously less than one full percent below trend.

The fourth quarter of 2007 was the last quarter in the sample period when the natural log of real GDP was not only less than one percent below trend but also less than two percent below trend (when estimating the trend using observations from the first quarter of 2001 through the fourth quarter of 2007). The gap variable GAP_01Q1_07Q4 was less than −0.020 (or in absolute value greater than +0.020) each quarter from the first quarter of 2008 through the second quarter of 2016. The gap of real GDP below its pre-recession trend widened most quarters through the end of the sample period. In the second quarter of 2009, the last quarter of the Great Recession, GAP_01Q1_07Q4 reached around −0.09462, implying that real GDP was roughly nine percent below its trend. Despite real GDP growing most quarters after the second quarter of 2009, the growth was inadequate to return real GDP back to its pre-Great-Recession trend by the second quarter of 2016, with real GDP approximately fourteen percent below its estimated trend in that quarter. The gap variables GAP_47Q1_16Q2, GAP_47Q1_07Q4, and GAP_01Q1_07Q4 are depicted from the first quarter of 2000 through the second quarter of 2016 in Fig. 3.3.

We may expect that real GDP in total in an economy would normally grow over time due to increases in population and improvements in technology. Is the slowdown in real GDP growth after the Great Recession due to a decrease in the population growth rate only? Further, this book is concerned with living standards, among other things. Per capita real GDP provides a better measure of the average living standard than does real GDP, although it does not necessarily provide adequate information about the median income per person or about distributional considerations. Nonetheless, to address whether what appears to have been either a break in the trend of real GDP or some other type of change in the

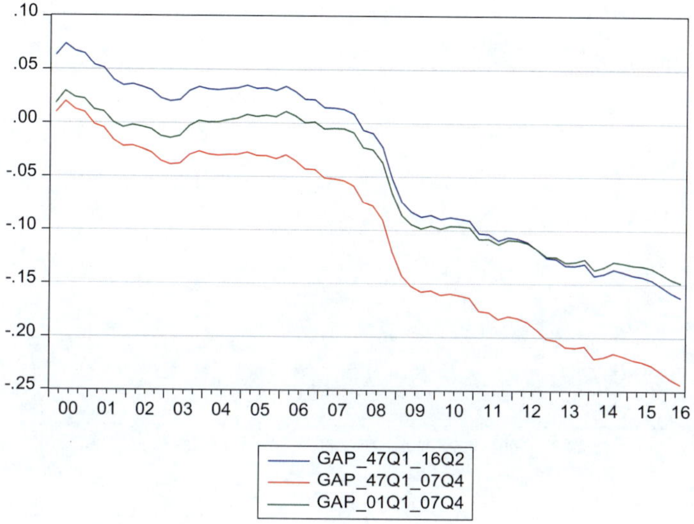

Fig. 3.3 Estimated 'gap variables' from the first quarter of 2000 through the second quarter of 2016 showing the actual natural log of quarterly U.S. real GDP (annualized and seasonally adjusted) minus its estimated trend with the trend estimated using observations (1) from the first quarter of 1947 through the second quarter of 2016 (GAP_47Q1_16Q2), (2) from the first quarter of 1947 through the fourth quarter of 2007 (GAP_47Q1_07Q4), and (3) from the first quarter of 2001 through the fourth quarter of 2007 (GAP_01Q1_07Q4) (*Sources* www.economagic.com, U.S. Bureau of Economic Analysis, Saint Louis Federal Reserve Bank, and the author's calculations)

trend was due solely to changes in population or its growth rate and to begin to address living standards, let's also look at per capita real GDP data, or real GDP per person.

Figure 3.4 shows the natural log of U.S. per capita real GDP over the entire sample period (the first quarter of 1947 through the second quarter of 2016) and its trend based on all observations in the sample period. As a reminder, the total and per capita U.S. real GDP data were probably compiled by the U.S. Bureau of Economic Analysis, with the total real GDP data accessed from www.economagic.com and the per capita data accessed from the Saint Louis Federal Reserve Bank website FRED.

(The numbers on the vertical axes of the graphs with the natural log or natural logs of per capita series can be larger than the numbers on

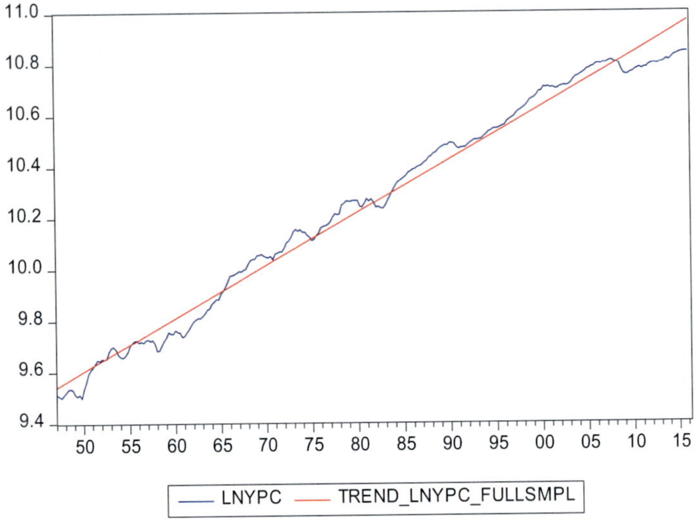

Fig. 3.4 Quarterly data for the natural log of U.S. per capita real GDP, annualized and seasonally adjusted, and the trend of the natural log of U.S. per capita real GDP from the first quarter of 1947 through the second quarter of 2016 (*Sources* Saint Louis Federal Reserve Bank FRED web page, U.S. Bureau of Economic Analysis, and the author's calculations)

the vertical axes of the graphs with the series showing the natural log or natural logs in total and not per capita form. The reason is that the per capita real GDP data are reported in actual dollars, but the total real GDP data are reported in billions of dollars. Thus, before applying the natural log transformation, a value of slightly more than 51,200 in the series for per capita real GDP in the second quarter of 2016 implies that per capita real GDP was roughly 51,200 dollars in that quarter, but a value for total real GDP in the data of nearly 16,600 in the second quarter of 2016 implies that total real GDP was roughly 16.6 *trillion* dollars because the total real GDP data are reported in billions of dollars.

The natural log of 51,200, approximately 10.8 and approximately the log of per capita U.S. real GDP in the second quarter of 2016, is clearly larger than the natural log of 16,600, approximately 9.7, representing in rough terms the log of total U.S. real GDP in billions of dollars. Of course, the natural log of 16.6 trillion, representing real GDP in actual constant-buying-power dollars (rather than in billions of constant-buying-power dollars), 'is larger than the natural log of 51,200'.)

Per capita real GDP was just barely above its estimated full sample trend in the second quarter of 2008, the second quarter of the Great Recession, when using all observations from the first quarter of 1947 through the second quarter of 2016 to estimate the trend. In the third quarter of 2008, per capita real GDP fell below the trend estimated over the entire sample period, and it fell fairly sharply below trend in the fourth quarter of 2008, with the gap variable PC_GAP_47Q1_16Q2 at roughly −0.011 and −0.040 in those two quarters, and remaining below trend thereafter. Note that 'PC_' before 'GAP' in the name PC_GAP_47Q1_16Q2 and other gap variables in this chapter denotes a gap variable for per capita real GDP. Thus, 'PC' in this context does not stand for personal computer.

PC_GAP_47Q1_16Q2 continued to decrease most quarters afterward, reaching a value of nearly −0.124 in the second quarter of 2016. This implies that per capita real GDP was approximately twelve percent below its estimated trend in the second quarter of 2016. Given that this is per capita real GDP, imagine all of the additional goods and services each person in the U.S. would have been able to consume had the U.S. economy been able to return to its trend following the Great Recession so that it would have produced more than ten percent more per person on an annualized basis. In light of the fact that the estimate of the trend for per capita real GDP used all observations from the first quarter of 1947 through the second quarter of 2016, barring substantial supply disruptions, should it have been possible to produce an amount of per capita real GDP at least equal to its trend in quarters long after the end of the Great Recession as long as aggregate demand grew sufficiently? But, as we are seeing, a failure of real GDP to return to trend following recessions, some of which were induced by decreases in aggregate demand, has led to very long-lasting, if not permanent, negative consequences for the subsequent growth after recessions.

As noted above when using the natural log of total U.S. real GDP rather than the log of per capita U.S. real GDP, recessions can possibly cause breaks in the trend of the series for real GDP. Thus, it may be appropriate to use other estimates of trend in addition to the trend estimated with all of the observations from the first quarter of 1947 through the second quarter of 2016 when trying to determine whether real output in the U.S. returned to trend after a recession.

Figure 3.5 shows gap variables comparing the natural log of per capita U.S. real GDP with its trend estimated using observations (a) from the first quarter of 1947 through the second quarter of 2016, (b) from the first quarter of 1947 through the fourth quarter of 2007, (c) from the first quarter of 2001 through the fourth quarter of 2007, and (d) from the third quarter of 2000 through the fourth quarter of 2007. I estimated the trend through the fourth quarter of 2007 in the last three cases because the beginning of the Great Recession in the first quarter of 2008 could have caused a break in the trend of per capita real GDP. Further, I estimated the trend in the third case with data starting with the first quarter of 2001 because the beginning of the dot-com-bubble recession could have caused a break in the trend. I also estimated the trend of U.S. total real GDP for cases a, b, and c (including the full sample period) when calculating the gap variables shown in Fig. 3.3.

Regarding per capita U.S. real GDP, to those three cases I add case d, the estimation of trend from the third quarter of 2000 through the fourth quarter of 2007 because U.S. per capita real GDP also declined in the third quarter of 2000 in addition to declining in the first and third quarters of 2001. Further, the third quarter of the year 2000 was relatively soon before the dot-com-bubble recession. Although per capita real GDP fell in the third quarter of 2006 and the first quarter of 2007, I did not think that these quarters would be part of either the Great Recession or part of a separate recession given that (1) these quarters occurred at least four quarters before the beginning of the Great Recession, (2) the decreases in output per person represented decreases in per capita real GDP of less than ninety dollars per year on an annualized basis, and (3) total real GDP increased during these two quarters. However, the third quarter of the year 2000 plus at least one quarter in the year 2006 and at least one quarter in the year 2007 will be discussed as possible breaking quarters in a later chapter. (Readers may want to note that other quarters occurred in the sample period when per capita U.S. real GDP decreased but total U.S. real GDP increased.)

To show all four gap variables starting at levels at least equal to zero and to use the same period as shown in Fig. 3.3 for the gap variables using total real GDP, the results in Fig. 3.5 display the gap variables for per capita real GDP from the first quarter of 2000 through the second quarter of 2016. The results show that of these four cases in Fig. 3.5, the gap variable for per capita real GDP is always the most positive or the least negative (at least from the first quarter of 2000 through the

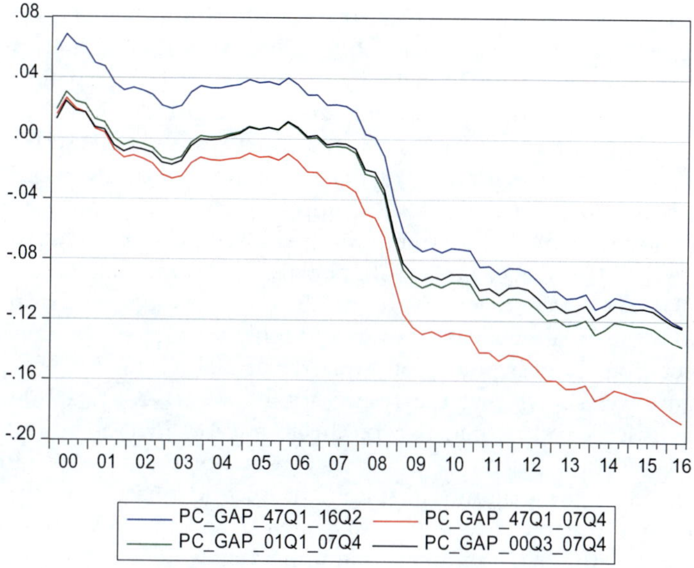

Fig. 3.5 Estimated 'gap variables' from the first quarter of 2000 through the second quarter of 2016 showing the actual natural log of quarterly U.S. per capita real GDP (annualized and seasonally adjusted) minus its estimated trend with the trend estimated using observations (1) from the first quarter of 1947 through the second quarter of 2016 (PC_GAP_47Q1_16Q2), (2) from the first quarter of 1947 through the fourth quarter of 2007 (PC_GAP_47Q1_07Q4), (3) from the first quarter of 2001 through the fourth quarter of 2007 (PC_GAP_01Q1_07Q4), and (4) from the third quarter of 2000 through the fourth quarter of 2007 (PC_GAP_00Q3_07Q4) (*Sources* Saint Louis Federal Reserve Bank FRED web page, U.S. Bureau of Economic Analysis, and the author's calculations)

second quarter of 2016) when the trend was estimated with data over the entire sample period (1947q1 through 2016q2). This implies that when allowing for breaks in the trend, the results about how far real output was below its trend were even greater.

As noted above, PC_GAP_47Q1_16Q2 last exceeded zero in the second quarter of 2008. By contrast, when estimating trend with observations from the first quarter of 1947 through the fourth quarter of 2007, the resulting gap variable PC_GAP_47Q1_07Q4 last exceeded zero in the second quarter of 2001 although its absolute value was again slightly less than 0.010 in the first quarter of 2005 and the first quarter of 2006 (although in terms of absolute value it was somewhat smaller in the third quarter of 2001). These absolute values less than 0.010 imply that per capita real output was only about one percent less than its estimated trend in those quarters. In the fourth quarter of 2007, the last quarter before the beginning of the Great Recession, PC_GAP_47Q1_07Q4 was approximately −0.035, implying that per capita real output stood roughly 3.5% below trend. With the start of the Great Recession, PC_GAP_47Q1_07Q4 grew more negative, implying further shortfalls of real GDP per person below its trend. The estimates suggest that per capita real GDP on an annualized basis was roughly seventeen percent below its pre-recession trend in the second quarter of 2016.

Figure 3.5 shows that the results for PC_GAP_47Q1_07Q4 are the least positive or most negative of the four cases in that figure, at least from the fourth quarter of 2000 (near but not quite the beginning of the period in the diagram) through the second quarter of 2016. With the two gap variables PC_GAP_47Q1_16Q2 and PC_GAP_47Q1_07Q4 representing the maximum and minimum values of the four variables, at least for most if not all of the quarters shown in Fig. 3.5, the other two gap variables PC_GAP_01Q1_07Q4 and PC_GAP_00Q3_07Q4 must be somewhere in between. After being above zero, below zero around and for a time after the dot-com-bubble recession and then back above zero, PC_GAP_01Q1_07Q4 and PC_GAP_00Q3_07Q4 were last greater than zero in the fourth quarter of 2006. Both of these gap variables were slightly below zero in each quarter of 2007, falling further below zero starting in the first quarter of 2008. With PC_GAP_00Q3_07Q4 at roughly −0.12454 and PC_GAP_01Q1_07Q4 at about −0.1371 in the second quarter of 2016, this implies that per capita real GDP was very roughly twelve percent and thirteen percent below each of the respective estimates of trend. This could suggest a considerable shortfall of production per person below potential in the U.S.

This also underscores the inability of the U.S. economy to return to its pre-recession growth trajectory, whether using total real GDP or per capita real GDP, within what many would likely consider a reasonable amount of time following the Great Recession. What kind of shock caused this departure of real GDP from the previous trend? I found using data from www.economagic.com showing a loss of real GDP most quarters from the first quarter of 2008 through the second quarter of 2009 plus a decrease in the price level (meaning deflation or inflation rates less than zero) in the second and third quarters of 2009. Using the reasoning that aggregate-demand-induced recessions lead to lower real GDP and lower inflation rates while aggregate-supply-induced recessions lead to lower real GDP but higher inflation, I and likely others would classify the Great Recession as being due to a negative AD shock. Also, financial crises such as the one around the beginning of the Great Recession are often associated with negative aggregate demand shocks.

This failure of the U.S. economy to return to its prior growth path following a decrease in aggregate *demand* appears completely incompatible with mainstream macroeconomic analysis, where prices and other factors adjust relatively quickly following changes in aggregate demand so that there should be neither a long-lasting departure of real output below its trend nor an output-reducing break in trend following a decrease in aggregate demand. Now, the question is 'Was the very long-lasting if not permanent reduction in real GDP growth following the negative AD shock in the form of the Great Recession an isolated event, or did at least one other decrease in aggregate demand cause either a long-term or a permanent decrease in the growth path of U.S. real output?'.

3.3 The Dot-Com-Bubble Recession

Readers may note that in Figs. 3.1 and 3.4, the logs of total and per capita U.S. real GDP were above their full-sample trends soon before the Great Recession. In fact, the output variables failed to fall below those full-sample trends due to the dot-com-bubble recession. The results in this chapter may suggest that the reason why total U.S. real GDP and per capita U.S. real GDP failed to fall below their full-sample trends soon after the dot-com-bubble recession is because the Great Recession and the Not-So-Great Recovery caused a substantial reduction in both of these estimated trends over the full sample period, perhaps to the point of breaking the trend lines. Allowing for downward breaks in trend before the Great Recession not only may be more appropriate statistically, but it helps to focus on the loss of well-being that people suffer when real GDP fails to return to its initial pre-recession trend. Therefore, I will not include full sample gap variables in figures to follow.

Additionally, the fact that filtered trends for the natural log of real output may not be helpful in determining whether a break in the *constant* trend of the log of an output variable (meaning no change in either the slope or the intercept of the trend line) has occurred (because the calculation of such filtered trends by their construction may substantially increase the likelihood that actual variable values are close to the filtered trend by allowing a *non-constant* trend) is one of the reasons why I did not use filtered variables in this chapter and in this book. If the gap variables of this chapter were calculated using a filtered trend, it may be much more likely that total and per capita real GDP would return to their reduced trends following a recession than when using a constant trend. Although Martin et al (2014) may not have been explicitly concerned with breaks in trend, their observation that when using filtered trends, output gaps caused by recessions are closed by reducing the filtered trend is a point that is at least similar to the point in the previous two sentences in this paragraph.

A downturn in equity prices occurred around the time of the dot-com-bubble recession, the last U.S. recession prior to the Great Recession. Obviously, this could have led to a negative wealth effect and in turn a reduction in spending. Increased private-sector leveraging in the 1990s and subsequent defaults, speculation in equity markets (some of which may not have been based on fundamentals), tighter monetary policy to stave off perceived inflation pressure, and other factors could have resulted in the dot-com-bubble recession in the U.S. in 2001. Given the slowdown in inflation in data from www.economagic.com (where quarter-to-quarter inflation (but annualized) fell from between 2.16% and 3.10% each quarter from 2000q1 through 2001q2 to below 1.30% each quarter from 2001q3 through 2002q1), the occurrence of a financial crisis (albeit less severe in at least some ways than the crisis around the Great Recession) with the bursting of the dot-com-bubble, and monetary policy tightening, the U.S. recession in 2001 appears to be more the result of a decrease in aggregate demand than a decrease in aggregate supply.

Was the U.S. economy in a situation where total real output was at least equal to the trend soon before the dot-com-bubble recession? Realizing that the Great Recession was associated with a change in the estimate of trend, none of the estimates of trend to be introduced beyond this point in this chapter will use all of the observations in the sample period (through the second quarter of 2016) to calculate the trend unless noted otherwise.

When estimating the trend with data from the first quarter of 1947 through the fourth quarter of 2000, the last quarter of the expansion before the dot-com-bubble recession, the natural log of actual real GDP last exceeded the estimated trend in the second quarter of 2000. Prior to that, the last time that the log of actual U.S. real GDP was greater than this estimate of trend was from the first quarter of 1985 through the second quarter of 1990. Nonetheless, (returning focus to the period near the dot-com-bubble recession) actual U.S. real GDP was less than one percent below the estimated trend in the fourth quarter of 1999, the first quarter of 2000, and the last two quarters of 2000 after being slightly above trend in the second quarter of 2000. The variable GAP_47Q1_00Q4 in Fig. 3.6 shows these data values starting with the first quarter of 2000.

Notice that with the onset of the dot-com-bubble recession in the first quarter of 2001, GAP_47Q1_00Q4 started to decrease at a faster rate. With GAP_47Q1_00Q4 reaching approximately −0.02 in the first quarter of 2001, real output was approximately two percent below its estimated pre-recession trend in that quarter. GAP_47Q1_00Q4 grew more negative most quarters afterward, reaching roughly −0.08 in the fourth quarter of 2007, the last quarter before the beginning of the Great Recession. We can infer from this estimate that total U.S. real GDP on an annualized basis was roughly eight percent below its pre-recession growth path the last quarter before the Great Recession struck. Figure 3.6 shows that in the last quarter of the sample period, GAP_47Q1_00Q4 was much further below the projection of trend estimated with data from the first quarter of the sample period through the fourth quarter of 2000 than this gap variable was below trend in the fourth quarter of 2007. In the second quarter of 2016, the gap variable takes on a value that translates to real GDP being roughly twenty-four percent below its trend.

As was the case when addressing whether real output in the U.S. returned to its pre-Great Recession trend after the Great Recession, I also estimate the trend for U.S. real GDP from the beginning of the previous recession (which occurred during part of 1990 and part of 1991) through the last quarter before the recession being analyzed for a possible post-recession return to trend. I do this because (a) Perron (1989) and others have noted that recessions (or at least shocks) could potentially be associated with breaks in trend, although Perron (1989) as discussed in Dornbusch et al. (2008, pp. 568–571) may have focused on the negative aggregate supply shock in 1973 as causing one break in the post-World War II period, and (b) Martin et al (2014) observed that negative-AD-shock-induced recessions may have long-term detrimental consequences for the growth of real GDP.

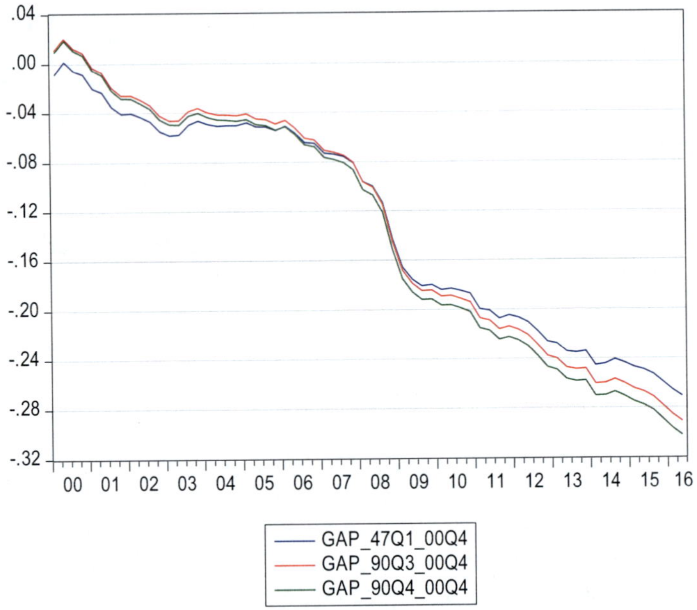

Fig. 3.6 Estimated 'gap variables' from the first quarter of 2000 through the second quarter of 2016 showing the actual natural log of quarterly U.S. real GDP (annualized and seasonally adjusted) minus its estimated trend with the trend estimated using observations (1) from the first quarter of 1947 through the fourth quarter of 2000 (GAP_47Q1_00Q4), (2) from the third quarter of 1990 through the fourth quarter of 2000 (GAP_90Q3_00Q4), and (3) from the fourth quarter of 1990 through the fourth quarter of 2000 (GAP_90Q4_00Q4) (*Sources* www.economagic.com, U.S. Bureau of Economic Analysis, Saint Louis Federal Reserve Bank, and the author's calculations)

It is not automatically clear which quarter is the best quarter to use as the start of the recession of 1990 and 1991. Data accessed in 2016 from www.economagic.com show that real GDP started to decrease in the fourth quarter of 1990. However, real GDP barely increased in the third quarter of 1990, and data accessed from www.economagic.com on July 20, 2013 show that real GDP decreased very slightly in the third quarter of 1990. Due to the uncertainty about which quarter is preferable to select as the beginning of the recession of 1990 and 1991, I estimate the trend with both the third quarter of 1990 and the fourth quarter of

1990 taking turns serving as the first quarter of the recession of 1990 and 1991.

The gap variables resulting from estimating the trend of U.S. real GDP from (a) the third quarter of 1990 through the fourth quarter of 2000 and (b) from the fourth quarter of 1990 through the fourth quarter of 2000, GAP_90Q3_00Q4 and GAP_90Q4_00Q4 respectively, were both greater than zero in the fourth quarter of 2000. Also, both of these two gap variables dropped below zero in the first quarter of 2001 and remained below zero permanently, at least through the end of the sample period, the second quarter of 2016. This suggests that actual real GDP in the U.S. failed to return to its pre-dot-com-bubble-recession trend by the second quarter of 2016 following the dot-com-bubble recession. These results are qualitatively similar to those for GAP_47Q1_00Q4 except GAP_47Q1_00Q4 fell below zero for the last time in the third quarter of 2000.

In the fourth quarter of 2007, GAP_90Q3_00Q4 was approximately –0.080, and GAP_90Q4_00Q4 was approximately −0.086, implying that U.S. real GDP was very roughly eight percent below its pre-recession trends when estimating trend starting either with the third or the fourth quarter of 1990 and going through the fourth quarter of 2000. As readers may expect, the shortfall of real U.S. output below its trend grew substantially during the Great Recession and the Not-So-Great Recovery, with GAP_90Q3_00Q4 falling to about −0.29 in the second quarter of 2016, and GAP_90Q4_00Q4 declining to around −0.30 in that quarter. This suggests that U.S. real GDP was very roughly twenty-five or twenty-six percent below its pre-dot-com-bubble-recession trend.

Were the post-dot-com-bubble-recession shortfalls of real GDP below its trend estimated with data from before the dot-com-bubble recession due only to changes in population? The short answer to the question is 'no.' All three gap variables using per capita U.S. real GDP and estimating the trend of real GDP per person in the U.S. through the fourth quarter of 2000 whether the trend estimation started with data in the first quarter of 1947 (PC_GAP_47Q1_00Q4), the third quarter of 1990 (PC_GAP_90Q3_00Q4), or the fourth quarter of 1990 (PC_GAP_90Q4_00Q4) were last greater than zero in the fourth quarter of 2000 as shown in Fig. 3.7 and fell below zero permanently (at least through the second quarter of 2016) in the first quarter of 2001.

Figures 3.6 and 3.7 show the gap variables, calculated with the natural logs of total U.S. real GDP and per capita U.S. real GDP, with the gap

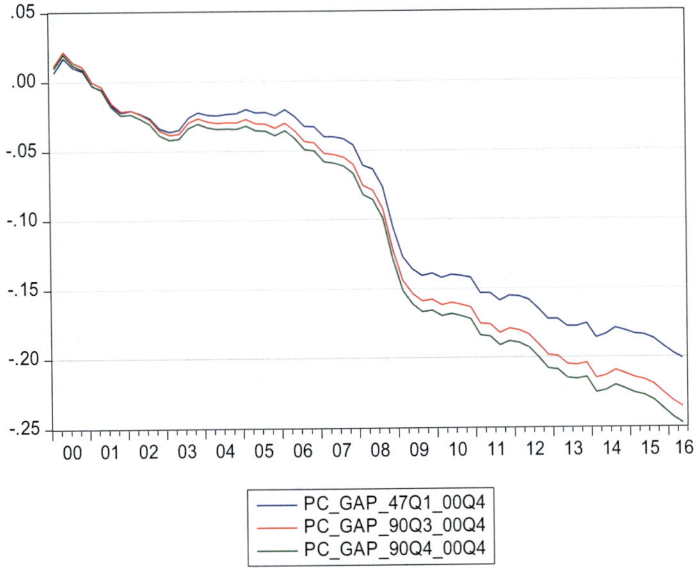

Fig. 3.7 Estimated 'gap variables' from the first quarter of 2000 through the second quarter of 2016 showing the actual natural log of quarterly U.S. per capita real GDP (annualized and seasonally adjusted) minus its estimated trend with the trend estimated using observations (1) from the first quarter of 1947 through the fourth quarter of 2000 (PC_GAP_47Q1_00Q4), (2) from the third quarter of 1990 through the fourth quarter of 2000 (PC_GAP_90Q3_00Q4), and (3) from the fourth quarter of 1990 through the fourth quarter of 2000 (PC_GAP_90Q4_00Q4) (*Sources* Saint Louis Federal Reserve Bank FRED web page, U.S. Bureau of Economic Analysis, and the author's calculations)

variable quarters in the figures spanning from the first quarter of 2000 through the second quarter of 2016. In summary, the figures show that each of the gap variables in the figure was greater than zero shortly before the recession that began in the first quarter of 2001. This implies that in each case depicted, total real GDP and per capita real GDP were above their estimated trends before the dot-com-bubble recession started. The figures also show that after the gap variables dropped below zero, they clearly failed to return to zero or positive values before the beginning of the Great Recession, probably growing more negative many quarters prior to the Great Recession.

Perhaps this was similar to the results from the previous subsection analyzing the Great Recession, except that no additional recession occurred after the end of the Great Recession through the second quarter of 2016, the last quarter in the sample period (so that the COVID-19-associated recession is not part of the sample period). These results seem to provide two cases of recessions resulting from decreases in aggregate demand where real GDP failed to return to its pre-recession trend within what many would likely consider a reasonable amount of time. Additionally, note that the gap variables for the dot-com-bubble recession in Figs. 3.6 and 3.7 tended to grow more negative after the commencement of the Great Recession. Discussions of additional gap variables for other recessions in the sample period are in the online appendix of the book.

3.4 Recap and Preparatory Remarks for the Next Chapter

In summary, Chapter 2 briefly reviewed major schools of macroeconomic thought and some empirical work about negative shocks, both providing context about how different views of the duration of decreases in real output growth due to decreases in aggregate demand fit into macroeconomic analysis. Afterward, the present chapter and its appendix presented analysis of the impact of ten recessions in the sample period, unable to find quarterly trends prior to the recession in 1947, an eleventh recession.

More specifically, most of the analysis included multiple estimates of pre-recession trend, varying based on (1) whether the estimate of trend started with the first quarter of the sample period (so that, in many if not most cases, the estimate of trend covers at least two recessions and two subsequent expansions in their entirety) or a later quarter, (2) the last quarter of data used to estimate trend, and (3) whether the natural logarithm of U.S. total real GDP or the log of U.S. per capita real GDP provided the data for estimating trend. Regarding the first two differences, in at least a few cases, this chapter and its appendix presented findings based on different starting quarters for a recession or different ending quarters of an expansion. Each estimate of trend was then subtracted from the natural log of either total real GDP or per capita real output, as appropriate, to find a gap variable.

A positive value in a quarter for a gap variable indicated that real output, either total or per person, exceeded its estimated trend, while a negative value suggested that real output was below trend. The gap variables usually if not always were approximately equal to zero soon before the recession being analyzed began.

The main question was, given that the gap variables suggested that real output was at least very roughly equal to its pre-recession trend in most cases soon before each of the ten recessions analyzed in this chapter began, did the gap variables, after dropping below zero in most cases around the onset of the recession being analyzed, return to exceeding or at least equaling zero either before the beginning of the next recession or the end of the sample period? In many cases, including the cases of the dot-com-bubble recession in 2001 and the Great Recession in 2008 and part of 2009, the answer is no. This implies that real GDP failed to return fully to its pre-recession trends following the beginnings of many recessions, including in some cases (though certainly not all cases) where decreases in aggregate demand likely caused recessions.

Although this study focused on data from the U.S., this finding is consistent with findings such as those by Martin et al. (2014), although it clearly contradicts the view in mainstream macroeconomics that negative aggregate demand shocks cannot have either a permanent or an essentially permanent impact on future real GDP. In the traditional view, only negative aggregate supply shocks can have a permanent or an essentially permanent negative impact on future real GDP. Is that view supported by the data? Do the findings of this section and those such as in Martin et al. (2014) suggest that the U.S. economy in at least one sense may not have fully recovered from some recessions including some of those induced by negative AD shocks? Further, do the results for per capita real GDP indicate that changes in population were not the only reason for real output failing to return to trend in the cases discussed above?

Based on gap variable analysis, Table 3.1 summarizes whether real GDP returned to its pre-recession trend either before the beginning of the next recession or by the end of the sample period (the latter in the case of the Great Recession) for each recession identified in this study from the recession of 1949 through the Great Recession. Unlike the discussion above and in the online appendix, the recessions as listed in Table 3.1 below are in chronological order from first to last.

Below that, Table 3.2 lists approximations for the constant term and the coefficient for the time trend term from regression equations used to calculate the gap variables in this chapter for the dot-com-bubble recession and the Great Recession. Estimates for many of the regression equations from earlier recessions appear in a table in the Chapter 2 appendix. Note that the calculations as listed in Table 3.2 are estimates with a maximum of five digits to the right of the decimal, but more than five digits after the decimal were used to calculate the gap variables in this chapter.

Regarding the results summarized in Table 3.1, total U.S. real GDP returned to its pre-recession trend in at least one method for estimating the trend used in this chapter during only three of ten recessions for which I was able to estimate a pre-recession trend using quarterly data. Two of those three recessions (1949q1–1949q4 and 1959q3–1960q4) seem to be mainly due to negative aggregate demand shocks, while the third (1969q4–1970q4) was an aggregate supply shock recession. The results for per capita real GDP were qualitatively similar except that one method used to estimate trend produced a gap variable for per capita real GDP finding that real output per person returned to trend following the recession from the third quarter of 1973 through the first quarter of 1975, an aggregate-supply-shock recession. Later negative AD shocks (the recession in 2001 following the bursting of the dot-com-bubble, the Great Recession in 2008 and 2009) produced shortfalls of the natural log of real GDP below its trend that persisted either until the next recession and then beyond or until the end of the sample period or both. (Readers may want to recall that except for the trend estimate for total and for per capita U.S. real GDP using the full sample period, when analyzing the Great Recession, none of the estimates of trend in this chapter included data through the second quarter of 2016.)

While there was an earlier negative AD shock (1953q3–1954q1) from which the economy in a sense did not fully recover before the beginning of the next recession, this could be due to a relatively short time from the last quarter of the recession (the first quarter of 1954) to the first quarter of the next recession (the first quarter of 1956). Between those two periods, data from www.economagic.com accessed November 2, 2016 show that during two quarters real GDP grew at an annualized rate faster than eight percent. Had the recession that started in 1956 not occurred, would real GDP have returned to trend after the recession of 1953 and 1954?

It may be worth noting that using the methodology in this chapter, before the energy crisis-related recessions of the mid-1970s and the early 1980s, the U.S. economy returned to trend in at least one method for estimating trend following not only two of the three negative AD shocks but also following one of the two negative AS shocks. However, starting with the energy crisis-related recessions, the natural log of total real GDP failed to return to its pre-recession trend after each recession (not including the COVID-19 recession) regardless of whether it was caused by an AS shock or an AD shock but (1) with the exception of one trend estimate for per capita real GDP for the earlier energy crisis recession and (2) with the caveat that per capita real GDP may have been somewhat close to returning to pre-recession trend following the early 1990s recession.

Does further statistical evidence exist to suggest that an economy does not necessarily fully recover from a decrease in aggregate demand? More specifically, can a decrease in aggregate demand cause a break in trend, thus slowing the growth of estimates of long-run equilibrium real output? Further, could any econometric issues cloud the analysis?

Regarding the last question, recall that Nelson and Plosser (1982), according to Dornbusch et al., (2008, pp. 567–569) and Hamilton (1994, p. 444), found that the series for real output had a unit root or was difference stationary. This statistical property could have important ramifications for the inferences that we can draw from econometric analysis. Further, many if not all of the regressions in this chapter had error terms with serial correlation, where knowing the error term in one quarter provided information that could help in predicting the error term in another quarter. Chapter 4 addresses these econometric issues more fully. If the analysis to follow in Chapter 4 and beyond produces results similar to the results from this chapter, then we could be in for a very long wait indeed for real GDP and its natural log to return to their pre-Great Recession trends. Many people either had to cut back on consumption or were unable to reach their full productive potential or both in light of the inability to return real GDP back to its pre-Great Recession trend.

After the Great Recession and initially expansionary fiscal policies, were policymakers waiting for prices and other factors to adjust and return real output to trend? Or, given that textbook-style analysis notes that expansionary monetary policy will be of limited help in increasing real output when an economy is close to a liquidity trap, was it an unwillingness to do the things necessary to return the economy back to trend, where in mainstream thinking it would presumably be getting the maximum sustainable production given the technology and resources available (perhaps assuming that the economy was at that level before the

Great Recession)? If inadequate aggregate demand was a problem then that could have been solved with more expansionary policies.

Table 3.1 Summary of results for U.S. recessions as defined in this book from the recession of 1949 through the Great Recession as to whether the natural logs of total U.S. real GDP and per capita U.S. real GDP returned to their pre-recession trends before the next recession (or by the second quarter of 2016 in the case of the Great Recession)

Recession	*Total*	*Per capita*
1949q1–1949q4	Yes	Yes
1953q3–1954q1	No	No
1956q1–1958q1	No	No
1959q3–1960q4	Yes 1, N/A 1**	Yes 1, N/A 1**
1969q4–1970q4	Yes 1, No 1***	Yes 1, No 1***
1973q1–1975q1	No	Yes 1, No 1***
1980q2–1982q3	No	No
1990q4–1991q1#	No	No But <0.5% Some Est. ##
2001q1–2001q3	No	No
2008q1–2009q2	No*	No*

Recessions starting in the following quarters are considered aggregate-supply-shock recessions: 1956q1, 1969q4, 1973q3, and 1980q2; the one starting 1990q4 was more difficult to categorize but was probably an AD-shock recession. The other recessions in the table are considered aggregate-demand-shock recessions. Also, I was unable to determine a pre-recession trend with quarterly data for the recession that started in or was already occurring in 1947q2.

No recession occurred after the second quarter of 2009 through the second quarter of 2016, the end of the sample period. Therefore, the entries of 'No' in the table above in the row for the Great Recession (2008q1–2009q2) mean that in both cases (estimating the trend using data (1) from the first quarter of 1947 through the fourth quarter of 2007 and (2) from the first quarter of the previous recession through the fourth quarter of 2007), neither the natural log of total U.S. real GDP nor the log of per capita U.S. real GDP returned to its pre-recession trend before the end of the sample period

**One of two estimates of the gap variable returned to a positive value for at least one quarter after the recession and before the next recession, but the other estimated gap variable failed to drop below zero as a result of the recession and thus the possibility of a return to pre-recession trend was not applicable

***One of two estimates of the gap variable returned to a positive value for at least one quarter after the recession and before the next recession, but the other estimated gap variable did not

#Data accessed in July 2013 indicate that the recession started in the third quarter of 1990

##Although the gap variables for per capita real output failed to exceed zero after the recession of 1990 and 1991, two of the four gap variables calculated for per capita real output were temporarily (in the second quarter of 2000) less than 0.004 further below zero than those gap variables were in the third quarter of 1990, the last quarter before total real GDP began to decrease. In other words, in two of the four cases, the actual natural log of per capita real GDP was not much further below trend in the second quarter of 2000 than it was in the third quarter of 1990

Source www.economagic.com, Saint Louis Federal Reserve Bank, U.S. Bureau of Economic Analysis, and the author's calculations

Table 3.2 Approximate values of the constant term (or the intercept) and the coefficient for the time trend over various selected time spans estimated to calculate gap variables for the dot-com-bubble recession and the Great Recession

Recession *Trend span*	*Total Real GDP const*	*Trend*	*Per Capita GDP const*	*Trend*
	Dot Com Bubble			
47q1-00q4	7.61639	0.00856	9.50667	0.00555
90q4-00q4	7.43769	0.00932	9.33989	0.00632
	Great Recession			
47q1-16q2	7.66372	0.00800	9.54085	0.00515
47q1-07q4	7.62653	0.00843	9.51177	0.00549
01q1-07q4	7.90095	0.00709	9.66234	0.00476

Sources www.economagic.com, Saint Louis Federal Reserve Bank, U.S. Bureau of Economic Analysis, and the author's calculations

References

Dornbusch, R., Fischer, S., & Startz, R. (2008). *Macroeconomics* (10th ed.). McGraw-Hill Irwin.

Hamilton, J. D. (1994). *Time series analysis*. Princeton University Press.

Martin, R. F., Munyan, T., & Wilson, B. A. (2014, November 12). *Potential output and recessions: Are we fooling ourselves*? IFDP Notes. Board of Governors of the Federal Reserve System. https://doi.org/10.17016/2573-2129.06. http://www.federalreserve.gov/econresdata/notes/ifdp-notes/2014/potential-output-and-recessions-are-we-fooling-ourselves-20141112.html

Nelson, C. R., & Plosser, C. I. (1982). Trends and random walks in macroeconomic time series: Some evidence and implications. *Journal of Monetary Economics, 10*(2), 139–162.

Perron, P. (1989). The great crash, the oil price shock, and the unit root hypothesis. *Econometrica, 57*, 1361–1401.

U.S. Bureau of Economic Analysis. (2016, November 2). *Real gross domestic product per capita [A939RX0Q048SBEA]*. Retrieved from FRED, Federal Reserve Bank of St. Louis. https://fred.stlouisfed.org/series/A939RX0Q048SBEA

www.economagic.com

CHAPTER 4

Econometric Issues To Consider and Model Selection for Some Hypothesis Tests

Abstract This chapter discusses standard regression assumptions such as uncorrelated residuals, constant variance of the residuals that are independently distributed, normally distributed residuals with zero mean, and the use of stationary variables. Given concerns about violations of standard regression assumptions in Chapter 3 regressions, this chapter introduces equations less likely to violate such assumptions. Rather than use either total real GDP or per capita real GDP in log level form, many if not most of the regression equations in this chapter and subsequent chapters use the first difference in the log of the output variable (or the 'change in' the output variable) on the left side of the regression equation and the right side of the regression equation. The goals are to avoid spurious regressions and to reduce if not eliminate serial correlation. Such violations of standard regression assumptions could invalid t-statistic and F-statistic hypothesis tests. This chapter also discusses model selection for many of the hypothesis tests in Chapter 5.

Keywords Heteroskedasticity · Serial correlation · Normally distributed errors · Zero mean residuals · Real GDP · Per Capita Real GDP · Lags · Schwarz Criterion · Standard regression assumptions

H. C. Hartman, *Bad Breaks in Real GDP and Employment*,
https://doi.org/10.1007/978-3-031-57769-7_4

4.1 Brief Recap of Results from Previous Chapters and Introduction to the Current Chapter

Among other things, the previous chapter used a relatively simple method for estimating the growth paths meaning the growth trajectories or the trends of the natural logs of real GDP and per capita real output in the U.S. The estimation of trend often started with the first quarter of the most recent previous downturn (before the recession being analyzed for a possible return to pre-recession trend) rather than the first quarter in the sample period. The empirical work did this to allow for the possibility of recessions causing multiple changes in trend or breaks in trend. In most cases, when analyzing the impact of a recession, the estimation of trend ended with the last quarter of data before that recession began. A key finding is that the Great Recession and at least two other negative-aggregate-demand-shock recessions (and more than one negative-aggregate-supply-shock recession) resulted in total and per capita real GDP failing to return to their pre-recession growth paths before the beginning of the next recession, or in the case of the Great Recession, before the end of the sample period.

The methodology of the previous chapter, seeking to make the findings and the message of this book comprehensible for the widest possible audience, was not sensitive to violations of standard econometric assumptions. Those will be addressed in this chapter.

As was the case with Chapter 3, much of the empirical work in this chapter and Chapter 5 does not use data beyond the end of the second quarter of 2016, and the data was accessed a while ago. Similar results for some of the hypothesis tests extending the sample period through the fourth quarter of 2019 and with the data accessed more recently appear toward the end of the book. Compared with results from the shorter sample period, some of the results with more observations may be somewhat less supportive of the view that decreases in aggregate demand can have very long-lasting consequences for real GDP, but some other results with the longer sample period could actually be more supportive of that hypothesis. This chapter often uses more advanced approaches to finding trend for hypothesis testing to increase confidence in the finding that decreases in aggregate demand can have long-lasting, if not permanent negative consequences for real GDP. However, hypothesis testing brings a set of issues, at least some of which will be addressed in this chapter.

4.2 Standard Regression Assumptions

Dougherty (2007, pp. 350–353, 387–390), Hamilton (1994, pp. 43–46, 202–227), and likely many others have discussed common assumptions in time series regressions. These assumptions include constant variance in the residuals or errors across the sample period (or homoskedasticity), independently distributed errors lacking serial correlation or autocorrelation, normally distributed (or 'bell-shaped curve') errors with zero mean, and the use of stationary variables in regressions.

Heteroskedasticity, serial correlation, regression residuals that are either not normally distributed or have a non-zero expected value (or both), and nonstationary variables in regressions violate these assumptions and present potential problems for hypothesis testing and conducting statistical inference. To provide a brief overview, heteroskedasticity refers to a non-constant variance of residuals, such that the variance of the residuals changes over the sample. Further, in time series analysis, regression residuals are often correlated with one or more other residuals. This implies that knowledge of the residual in a period (that is, a month or a quarter or a year) provides information helpful in predicting the value of another residual. Regression residuals could have a non-zero mean, be skewed above the mean or below the mean, be overly clustered around the mean or be insufficiently clustered around the mean, or exhibit some combination of these. Weakly stationary variables or covariance-stationary variables have constant unconditional means and constant unconditional variances. Nonstationary variables have either unconditional means or unconditional variances or both that vary over time.

All of these factors in the paragraph above could present problems for hypothesis testing. Readers should interpret the results with appropriately due caution.

Let's consider the issue of nonstationarity first. The use of models with nonstationary data could yield spurious regression results as noted by Hamilton (1994, pp. 557–562), Dougherty (2007, pp. 350, 387–390), and probably many others. For example, the use of nonstationary variables could impact t-test-statistic and F-test-statistic results, as per Hamilton (1994, p. 561) and Dougherty (2007, p. 388), with both the F-statistic and the t-statistic both tending to grow as the sample size grows with nonstationary data. (Note that the F-test should not be confused with receiving a grade of 'F' on a test!).

Given econometric concerns, in empirical results in Chapter 5 I will focus initially on breakpoint test results from versions of the models with differenced data and one lagged value of the left-side variable on the right side of the regression equation. Hamilton (1994, pp. 561–562) and likely many others have discussed using differenced data, or data in 'change in' form, as a method for preventing potentially spurious regressions that could arise from the use of nonstationary data in regressions. When starting with a series that in level or log level form is nonstationary, performing differencing a sufficient number of times, perhaps only once, likely makes the resulting series stationary.

My understanding based on Hamilton (1994, pp. 202–209, 215–217) and Dougherty (2007, pp. 71, 242, 350–351, 387–388) is that heteroskedasticity among the residuals, non-normality of residuals, a non-zero mean of the residuals, and serial correlation of residuals would imply that the F-test would have an unknown distribution, at least in non-infinite samples. Additionally, according to Hamilton (1994, pp. 215–217) and Dougherty (2007, p. 387), the estimated coefficients from an autoregression may be biased below their true values if the sample period is not infinite due to the use of lags in autoregressions. However, my understanding based on Hamilton (1994, pp. 209, 216, 416–417) and Dougherty (2007, pp. 350–353, 387–388) is that ordinary least squares regressions provide consistent estimates of the true parameter values despite the possible presence of heteroskedastic, serially correlated, and/or non-normally distributed residuals *as long as both (1) the regression residuals are not correlated with the right-side variables in the regression equation and (2) the variables in the regression exhibit weak persistence, the latter often interpreted as a practical matter to mean that the regression variables are stationary*. Consistent estimates converge to one value, the true population value, as the sample size approaches infinity, despite possible bias in finite samples.

Given that (1) in the cases in this book that I have checked, the correlations and covariances between the residual in period t and the right-side variables corresponding to the left-side variables (for example, in Chow breakpoint testing in Chapter 5, the output variable from period t-1 on the right side of the equation for the output variable in period t on the left side) in the regression equations are essentially zero (with absolute values less than $1.0*10^{-10}$ in most if not all cases), and (2) the output variables in regression Models A and B use differenced total real GDP data and differenced per capita real GDP data (both in natural log form prior to differencing) that appear stationary based on results from augmented Dickey–Fuller (1979) unit root tests *sans* a break; the estimated coefficients and constants may well be consistent. (Regarding the first point, an example of a type of regression equations that I may not have checked for a lack of correlation or covariance between the residuals and the regressors would be the equations from Chapter 3. Another example could be unit root test equations without breaks.) Because the estimated coefficients appear consistent, the estimated residuals should also be consistent. Thus, the Chow breakpoint tests may have validity at least asymptotically if not within finite sample periods. But I probably cannot claim consistency with absolute certainty given a caveat discussed in Sect. 4.4.

According to Hamilton (1994, pp. 417), the use of generalized least squares (GLS) provides a more efficient estimate (meaning an estimate subject to less variation) of parameters than ordinary least squares (OLS) when the resulting OLS residuals exhibit either serial correlation or heteroskedasticity. However, is my understanding of Hamilton (1994, pp. 220–223) correct that to use GLS, it may be necessary for the matrix created by multiplying the vector of OLS residuals by the transpose of the vector of OLS residuals (resulting in a T*T matrix (if the residuals vector is T*1)) to be invertible? Having had difficulty inverting the matrix constructed from OLS residuals for Models A and B over the full sample period, I will leave GLS estimation for future possible work.

Consistent but possibly biased and possibly inefficient estimates of the parameters and the residuals that may be valid only asymptotically may be the best achievable result given the likelihood of biased estimates in autogregressions noted by Hamilton (1994, pp. 215–217) and Dougherty (2007, p. 387) and the possible inability to use GLS with Models A and B over the sample period. My understanding is that bias exists regardless of whether or not the residuals are heteroskedastic, serially correlated, or non-normally distributed.

Further, to the extent that the estimates are biased due to the presence of lagged variable values in the autoregressions, Dougherty (2007, p. 363) notes that the bias is forgotten as a practical matter in the absence of autocorrelation. In light of the facts that (1) the Chow breakpoint test *F*-statistics (and most if not all of the other statistics) will be asymptotically valid as long as one or more caveats do not apply and (2) my understanding based on Hamilton (1994, pp. 205, 213–214) and the *EViews 10 Users' Guide II* (2017, p. 188) is that the Wald statistic is asymptotically Chi-squared distributed despite possible violations of standard assumptions about regression residuals; much of the remaining discussion of possible heteroskedasticity, serial correlation, and non-normality of residuals will be in the appendix. Readers should be aware that at least some results may be valid only from an asymptotic perspective.

Correspondingly, readers should not place excessive confidence in either the estimates of parameters or in the hypothesis test results in light of the econometric issues discussed above and in light of possible model misspecification issues such as the possible failure to include important variables on the right sides of regression equations. For example, perhaps at least one additional lagged change in the output variable should appear on the right side of regression equations. Additionally, maybe another variable such as a measure of the money stock should be included in the regression. Further, perhaps another type of hypothesis testing would be more appropriate. In sum, maybe it would be best to view the results as an approximation or an illustration.

4.3 Some Notes About Testing with Data in First Difference Form

As was the case in the last chapter, the data for total U.S. real GDP were compiled by the U.S. Bureau of Economic Analysis (BEA) and were accessed from an earlier version of the website www.economagic.com (but may have been obtained through the Saint Louis Federal Reserve), while the per capita U.S. real GDP data were also compiled by the U.S. Bureau of Economic Analysis (2016) but were accessed from the FRED web page of the St. Louis Federal Reserve Bank. The two series were accessed on November 2, 2016. The sample period ends with the second quarter of 2016 based in part on data availability as work progressed on the manuscript for this book. Again, results with an extended sample period through the fourth quarter of 2019 for some of the work appear in Chapter 7.

Many of the hypothesis tests in the next chapter use the first differences of the natural logs of total U.S. real GDP and per capita U.S. real GDP. Given that many including Nelson and Plosser (1982) according to Hamilton (1994, p. 444) and Dornbusch et al. (2008, pp. 567–569), have found real output to have a unit root or to be difference stationary, the problems of hypothesis testing using series with unit roots could plague hypothesis tests in this chapter if the tests were to use series with unit roots. I do not know if spurious regressions would not be a problem in a univariate setting for the hypothesis tests in this book with data in level or log level form. In first difference form or 'change in' form, the natural logs of both total U.S. real GDP and per capita U.S. real GDP may be stationary or I(0), lacking unit roots, based on results from the augmented Dickey–Fuller (1979) test (without any breaks). Thus, using differenced data very likely enhances the validity of hypothesis testing.

A potential problem with this approach is that the level of real output is important but that differencing may possibly render one type of break more difficult to detect. For example, consider a hypothetical break in the trend of the natural log of real GDP, not differenced, that shows up in the output series as a parallel downward shift in the trend of the natural log of real GDP. If the real output series is in differenced form, then from the perspective of hypothesis testing, would a permanent downward shift in the intercept of the *level* of the log of the real output series be detectable in the *first difference* of the log of the real output series? Or, if the parallel downward shift in the level version of the series appears in the differenced data as a relatively large negative value for the quarter or the relatively few quarters in which the downward shift occurred, then would that cause breakpoint tests using differenced data to be unable to detect a permanent break in any of those quarters? The differencing process may make it less likely to find evidence of breaks in hypothesis tests.

However, given the findings of others such as Martin et al. (2014) and given the findings in Chapter 3, any additional evidence supporting the view that changes in aggregate demand could cause breaks in trend could strengthen confidence in the thinking that negative aggregate demand shocks can potentially have essentially permanent, if not totally permanent, negative impacts on real output. Total real GDP and per capita real GDP may be important in level (or log level) form, not only in first difference form. But, is there statistically valid evidence of a change in the U.S.-real-output-generating process? To the extent that the results from Chapter 3 are valid, do those results show that the level of U.S. real output after a recession, both in total and per capita, often though not always failed to meet projections based on pre-recession trends? Later in Chapter 5, I also consider breakpoint unit root tests where the left-side variable and at least one variable on the right side of the test regression equation are in log level form. A further discussion about possible advantages and disadvantages of the different approaches in testing for breaks, used in this chapter with data in log level form versus data in 'change in the log of' form, appears later.

The next section begins with model selection and unit root testing. Then, in Chapter 5 I present results from hypothesis testing in differenced form. The first set of tests will be Chow (1960) breakpoint tests. Wald coefficient restriction tests and t-statistic intercept tests (where the intercept under the null hypothesis is the intercept from another subsample period rather than zero) provide additional forms of hypothesis testing. However, most of these t-statistic tests are in the appendix. Given that the data are in 'first difference of the natural log of' form, am I correct in thinking that econometric evidence of a break in the intercept (again with data in 'change in the log of' form) *could* suggest a likely break in the trend coefficient when the data are in log level form?

In part due to the point above about what could be an inability to test for a permanent downward shift in the level of the log of real output when using differenced data, I also consider unit root tests that allow for one breakpoint. These unit root tests with a break are preceded by Chow forecast tests.

4.4 Model Selection, Differencing, and a Caveat

Often in time series econometrics, including on the right side of a regression equation one or more lagged values of the dependent variable improves the fit of the regression, reduces serial correlation, and the lagged values could have statistical significance. Further, when a measure of real output is the dependent variable on the left side of the equation, the inclusion of at least one lagged value of the output variable on the right side of the regression equation could help to explain cyclical fluctuations. Thus, I include at least one lagged value of the real output variable on the right sides of many if not all of the regression equations for Chow breakpoint tests. Most of the regression equations in this chapter and in subsequent chapters have a constant or an intercept term, with these two terms being synonymous. At least a few augmented Dickey–Fuller (1979) unit root test equations in the online appendix may not have any intercept terms. Some of the regression equations in this chapter and subsequent chapters may also include a time trend.

The centered R-squared and adjusted R-squared statistics exceed 0.999 with two lags when the data is in log level, un-differenced form, and a time trend is included, indicating a good fit for the regressions, given that the maximum R-squared statistic is 1.0. Thus, it seems that, at least for the models in log level form, adding other variables to the right side of the regression equations could not increase either the R-squared statistic or the adjusted R-squared statistic by much.

But econometric concerns have led me to focus initially on breakpoint test results from versions of the model with output data differenced after applying the natural log transformation. Often, differencing data once can remove nonstationarity from a variable with a unit root. To ensure relatively parsimonious regression models, I regress the real output variable on no lagged values through five lagged values of the real output variable on the right side of regression equations. When using differenced data, the use of one lagged output variable value from the quarter before produces regressions with the smallest Schwarz (1978) criterion, as shown in Table 4a.1 in the Chapter Four Appendix. Because the model with only one lagged difference minimizes the Schwarz (1978) criterion or maximizes the absolute value of the Schwarz (1978) criterion, I focus (at least initially) on the model with just one lag of the output variable. This is the structure comparable to the version of the model mentioned in the paragraph above with two lagged variable values from the previous two quarters when the data are in log level, un-differenced form. Readers may want to note that I decided to use the approach of minimizing the Schwarz (1978) criterion rather than minimizing the Akaike (1974) Information Criterion when selecting the lag structure at least in part due to a desire for parsimony.

Equations 4.1 and 4.2 display the two regression models with differenced data. The variable $DLNY_t$ represents the first difference of the natural logarithm of total U.S. real GDP in quarter t (or the log of total U.S. real GDP in a quarter minus the log of total U.S. real GDP from the prior quarter), while the variable $DLNY_{t-1}$ shows the same variable except that it is from the previous quarter, quarter $t-1$. The variables $DLNYPC_t$ and $DLNYPC_{t-1}$ are very similar except they refer to the log differences of per capita U.S. real GDP in periods t and $t-1$, respectively.

The regression residual from Model A in time period t is given by ε_{At} (not to be confused with the word 'eat'), while the regression residual from Model B is denoted by ε_{Bt}. I use the Chow (1960) breakpoint test to test for breaks with emphasis on hypothesized breaks in the constants or intercepts of Models A and B, C_A and C_B. The parameters β_A and β_B in Eqs. 4.1 and 4.2 are estimated coefficients that are multiplied by the change in the log of the output variable one quarter earlier. These products contribute to the determination of the change in the log of the output variable in each of the two models.

$$\text{DLNY}_t = C_A + \beta_A * \text{DLNY}_{t-1} + \varepsilon_{\text{A}t} \quad \text{(Model A)} \qquad (4.1)$$

$$\text{DLNYPC}_t = C_B + \beta_B * \text{DLNYPC}_{t-1} + \varepsilon_{\text{B}t} \quad \text{(Model B)} \qquad (4.2)$$

The regression models include a constant and use ordinary least squares unless noted otherwise. As noted above, I focus initially on regression models with one lagged change in the real output variable based on Schwarz (1978) criterion results. Readers can find a summary of regression results from the two models in Table 4.1. Please note that, in light of possible asymptotic validity, no adjustments were made to the standard errors, *t*-statistics, or *p*-values in Table 4.1 or elsewhere in this book unless noted otherwise, despite possible violations of standard regression assumptions.

Readers can find results both over what is essentially the full sample period and also over ten subsample periods of heteroskedasticity tests based on the work of Breusch and Pagan (1979), Godfrey (1978), and Koenker (1981), and White (1980) in the online appendix of the current

Table 4.1 Summary of regression results of the two models over the full sample period

	Intercept (C) *(standard error)* T-*statistic* (p-*value)*	*Slope coefficient (β)* *(standard error)* T-*Statistic* (p-*value)*	*Eqn.* R^2 *Eqn. Adj.* R^2 *Eqn. SSR* *Eqn. SC*
Model A (Eq. 4.1) Total	0.004893 (0.000687) 7.121405 (0.0000)	0.372611 (0.055982) 6.655946 (0.0000)	0.139181 0.136040 0.021383 −6.586959
Model B (Eq. 4.2)	0.003068 (0.000594) 5.163489 (0.0000)	0.369243 (0.056011) 6.592370 (0.0000)	0.136897 0.133747 0.021178 −6.596572

The last column shows statistics for each equation (abbreviated Eqn.); R^2 represents *R*-squared, Adj. R^2 represents adjusted *R*-squared, SSR represents the sums of squared residuals, SC represents the Schwarz (1978) Criterion

Sources www.economagic.com, Saint Louis Federal Reserve Bank FRED web page, U.S. Bureau of Economic Analysis, Schwarz (1978) and the author's calculations

chapter. Also in the appendix are Breusch–Godfrey serial correlation LM test results and Jarque–Bera normality test results.

A caveat may be in order at this point. The possibility of finding at least one downward break in the intercept in the equation for the change in the natural log of real GDP either in per capita form or in total may suggest that at least one change in the unconditional mean of the output variable has occurred. My understanding of Hamilton (1994, pp. 45–46) is that a stationary variable has no change in its unconditional mean and no change in its unconditional variance. Thus, despite failing to find evidence of nonstationarity in the *first differences* of the natural logs of U.S. real GDP *en toto* and per person in augmented Dickey–Fuller (1979) unit root testing or Phillips–Perron (1988) unit root testing in the testing that I have done, do the findings of one or more breaks suggest that these two output variables, *both in first difference form*, were actually not stationary? If that is the case, then does the nonstationarity of these two variables cloud the analysis and cast doubt on how much confidence we can place in the conclusion of structural breaks? Is there an explanation for this? Are the results at least asymptotically consistent if the data are not stationary due to the possibility of at least one break? Is it circular to assume that a variable must be stationary meaning absolutely no possible breaks in mean or variance when conducting hypothesis testing but then to have tests for breaks which could identify breaks in the mean? Is this why I sometimes feel like I'm going in circles? Does this explain the circular flow diagram in economics? Is the assumption of stationarity important only for work with two or more different time series variables (not including univariate autoregressions)?

I cannot absolutely guarantee consistency and asymptotic validity in light of this caveat in the paragraph above. This caveat is one of the reasons why I consider breakpoint unit root test results in addition to results from other types of hypothesis tests in the next chapter.

References

Akaike, H. (1974). A new look at the statistical model identification. *IEEE Transactions on Automatic Control, 19*(6), 716–723.

Breusch, T. S., & Pagan, A. R. (1979). A simple test for heteroskedasticty and random coefficient variation. *Econometrica, 48*, 1287–1294.

Chow, G. C. (1960). Tests of equality between sets of coefficients in two linear regressions. *Econometrica, 28*(3), 591–605.

Dickey, D. A., & Fuller, W. A. (1979). Distribution of the estimators for autoregressive time series with a unit root. *Journal of the American Statistical Association, 74*, 427–431.

Dornbusch, R., Fischer, S., & Startz, R. (2008). *Macroeconomics* (10th ed.). McGraw-Hill Irwin.

Dougherty, C. (2007). *Introduction to Econometrics* (3rd ed.). Oxford University Press.

EViews 10 User's Guide II. (2017) IHS Global, Inc. Irvine, CA.

Godfrey, L. G. (1978). Testing for multiplicative heteroscedasticity. *Journal of Econometrics, 8*, 227–236.

Hamilton, J. D. (1994). *Time series analysis*. Princeton University Press.

Koenker, R. (1981). A note on studentizing a test for heteroskedasticity. *Journal of Econometrics, 17*, 107–112.

Martin, R. F., Munyan, T., & Wilson, B. A. (2014, November 12). *Potential output and recessions: Are we fooling ourselves?* IFDP Notes. http://www.federalreserve.gov/econresdata/notes/ifdp-notes/2014/potential-output-and-recessions-are-we-fooling-ourselves-20141112.html

Nelson, C. R., & Plosser, C. I. (1982). Trends and random walks in macroeconomic time series: Some evidence and implications. *Journal of Monetary Economics, 10*(2), 139–162.

Phillips, P. C. B., & Perron, P. (1988). Testing for a unit root in time series regression. *Biometrika, 75*, 335–346.

Schwarz, G. (1978). Estimating the dimension of a model. *Annals of Statistics, 6*, 461–464.

US. Bureau of Economic Analysis. (2016, November 2). *Real gross domestic product per capita [A939RX0Q048SBEA]*. Retrieved from FRED, Federal Reserve Bank of St. Louis; https://fred.stlouisfed.org/series/A939RX0Q048SBEA

White, H. (1980). A heteroskedasticity-consistent covariance matrix and a direct test for heteroskedasticity. *Econometrica, 48*, 817–838.

www.economagic.com

CHAPTER 5

Hypothesis Testing with Real GDP: Somewhat Mixed Results

Abstract Many of the hypothesis test results appear in this chapter of the book and the online-only appendix. The tests have attempted to correct for possible violations of standard regression assumptions. This chapter and its online appendix present Chow (1960) breakpoint test results and breakpoint unit root test results. This chapter also has Wald coefficient restriction test results and *t*-statistic test results seeking a change in the intercept over subsample periods. This chapter also offers Chow forecast test results. Although less clear than in Chapter 3, many of the results support the view that at least some negative aggregate demand shocks have resulted in downward breaks in U.S. real GDP in log level and 'change in the log of' form (with a unit root interpreted as a break in each period). Does a break in the intercept with data in 'change in the log of' form suggest a break in the time trend with log level data? At least one downward break in U.S. per capita output likely also occurred. This suggests that changes in population (or its growth rate) alone cannot explain all downward breaks in U.S. real output that seem to have been associated with decreases in aggregate demand.

Keywords Real GDP · Per capita real GDP · Chow breakpoint testing · Wald restriction testing · Chow forecast testing · Breakpoint unit root testing · *t*-statistic tests · Aggregate demand · Aggregate supply · Macroeconomics

H. C. Hartman, *Bad Breaks in Real GDP and Employment*,
https://doi.org/10.1007/978-3-031-57769-7_5

5.1 Chow Breakpoint Testing

We begin hypothesis testing for breaks with Chow (1960) breakpoint testing. Chow (1960) breakpoint tests help to determine whether a structural break occurred in one or more of the right-side terms of the regression equation. Given that the intercept (meaning the constant) in the regression equation with the data in 'change in the log of' form seems to be associated with the trend coefficient from a regression equation with the data in log level form, do any breaks found in the intercept with the data in change of in the log form suggest possible evidence of breaks in the trend coefficient with the data expressed in log level form? The data for total real GDP and per capita real GDP are from www.economagic.com and the U.S. Bureau of Economic Analysis (2016), respectively, unless noted otherwise.

Our main focus in Chow (1960) breakpoint testing is to look for evidence of breaks in the two real output series either when recessions as defined in this book start or near the beginnings of recessions, particularly negative-aggregate-demand-shock recessions. (Readers can refer to Table 3.1 for a list of the recessions.) The chance of finding more than one downward break in the sample period due to a negative AD shock could suggest that perhaps we should not be surprised if the Great Recession was associated with a permanent downward break in real output. Readers should realize that conducting the Chow (1960) breakpoint test for one or more breaks in the intercept only and not the coefficient may substantially increase the likelihood of finding breaks when compared with searching for breaks in both the intercept and any applicable coefficients. Readers should also realize that searching for breaks near the beginnings of recessions (rather than a one-time test in just one quarter) could possibly alter the distribution of the test statistic in ways that in at least some cases in this chapter may possibly not have been adequately considered.

For brevity, I will summarize the results from Chow breakpoint tests seeking a single break in the intercept to devote more attention in the body of the chapter to tests for joint breaks. Those interested can find more information about tests for a single break in the appendix. I did not seek evidence for a break in 1949 in these trials at least in part due to the return of total and per capita real GDP to trend following that recession using the methodology from Chapter 3.

Of the trials in the online appendix, tests for a single break in the intercept for Model A (with the change in the log of total U.S. real GDP) among the recession-starting quarters found evidence of a break at the ten percent level in seven of the nine quarters. Of those seven quarters, the evidence also existed at the five percent level for three quarters, with two of those quarters being the beginnings of negative-aggregate- demand-shock recessions, those starting in the first quarters of 2001 and 2008. Evidence suggests that the other quarter with significance at the five percent level, the third quarter of 1973, marked the start of a negative-aggregate-supply-shock recession.

Regarding Model B (with the change in the log of per capita U.S. real GDP), the finding of a single break in the intercept in a recession-starting quarter occurred in just two quarters of the ones that I tried, those being the first quarters of 2001 and 2008—and the significance was at the ten percent level but not at the five percent level. However, in cases where real output falls into recession more gradually by first increasing but at a slower rate than it increased previously before decreasing, it may be reasonable to test for breaks in quarters near but before the starts of recessions. Readers may wish to note that when testing for a single intercept break in Model B, the use of the third quarter of 2000 and the second quarter of 2006 find evidence of a break at the six percent level, while the use of the fourth quarter of 2007 finds evidence of a break at the 7.5% level. When applied instead to Model A, those quarters all produced evidence of a single intercept break at the five percent level. The use of the second quarter of 1973 produced evidence of a single intercept break at the five percent level in Model A, while evidence at the seven percent level for a single break was found in the second quarter of 1953. Those interested can find more in the online appendix.

Finding several quarters in different trials in which a single intercept break occurred could suggest that joint breaks occurred, meaning more than one intercept break occurred over the sample period within the same test trial. To that end, I have conducted test trials with sets of quarters over the full sample period, with each set comprised of at least two quarters. Focusing initially on a group of five trials in Table 5.1 first using Model A where each quarter in each set was the first quarter of a recession (as defined in this book), the tests find evidence of joint intercept breaks at the six percent level for three sets: Set 1 (comprised of the first quarters of 2001 and 2008), Set 2 (consisting of the third quarter of 1953, the first quarter of 2001, and the first quarter of 2008), and Set

3 (having the third quarter of 1973, the first quarter of 2001, and the first quarter of 2008). Readers may want to note that Set 2 has significance at the five percent level. Set 4, comprised of four quarters (1953q3, 1973q3, 2001q1, and 2008q1), finds evidence of four joint breaks in the intercept around the 7.0 or 7.25% level depending on the test statistic. Set 5 produces evidence of breaks at the eleven percent level.

Some other combinations in the appendix of this chapter find evidence of multiple breaks fairly near if not at the ten percent level, and two of those sets (with evidence somewhat near the ten percent level) have five quarters. These other sets are only in the appendix due in part to in most if not all cases at least one of the dummy variables used to allow a break in a particular quarter having a positive coefficient, while at this point

Table 5.1 Chow breakpoint test *p*-value results for multiple breaks in the constant in each test using the *F*-test and the Wald statistic for both Model A (total real GDP) and Model B (per capita real GDP)

Set	*Quarters*	*d.o.f*	*Model A values* F-*test*	*Wald*	*Model B values* F-*test*	*Wald*
Set 1	01q1 + 08q1	(2, 272)	0.0531*	0.0515*	0.1656	0.1637
Set 2	Set 1 + 53q3	(3, 271)	0.0481**	0.0460**	0.2045	0.2019
Set 3	Set 1 + 73q3	(3, 271)	0.0567*	0.0544*	0.2516	0.2492
Set 4	Set 2 + 73q3	(4, 270)	0.0722*	0.0692*	0.3174	0.3148
Set 5	Set 3 + 69q4	(4, 270)	0.1092	0.1059	0.3930	0.3909

Note that a single asterisk (*) denotes significance at the ten percent level, while two asterisks (**) denote significance at the five percent level

Note the following

Both numbers in parentheses apply to the degrees of freedom associated with the *F*-test statistic *p*-value for the set in each row. The first number in parentheses before the comma gives the degrees of freedom associated with the Wald statistic *p*-value for the set in that row. (The *F*-test statistics and Wald statistics appear in the appendix.) Also, note that regarding Set 5 with Model B, the estimated coefficient for the dummy variable for a break in the fourth quarter of 1969 was positive

The quarters in each set are spelled out below. When reading the table, it may help to realize that most rows refer to another set number and then add an additional quarter. For example, Set 2 has the same quarters as Set 1 (2001q1 and 2008q1) plus 1953q3

Set 1 has quarters 2001q1 and 2008q1

Set 2 has quarters 1953q3, 2001q1, and 2008q1

Set 3 has quarters 1973q3, 2001q1, and 2008q1

Set 4 has quarters 1953q3, 1973q3, 2001q1, and 2008q1

Set 5 has quarters 1969q4, 1973q3, 2001q1, and 2008q1

Sources www.economagic.com, Saint Louis Federal Reserve Bank FRED web page, U.S. Bureau of Economic Analysis, and the author's calculations

we are mainly interested in downward breaks with a negative coefficient). Tests in the appendix that I performed with six, seven, and nine recession-starting quarters failed to find evidence of joint breaks. Note that both Tables 5.1 and 5.2 as well as tables in the appendix have *F*-test statistics and Wald test statistics from EViews 10 software but do not include log likelihood ratio test statistics. In the tests conducted in this chapter, the log likelihood ratio statistics are usually somewhat more supportive of the hypothesis that one or more breaks occurred.

Table 5.2 Additional Chow breakpoint test *p*-value results (with alternate sets of quarters, in many cases, not-recession-initiating) for multiple breaks in the constant in each test using the *F*-test and the Wald statistics for both Model A (total real GDP) and Model B (per capita real GDP)

Set	*Quarters*	*d.o.f*	*Model A values* F-*Test*	*Wald*	*Model B values* F-*Test*	*Wald*
Set 1a	00q3 + 07q4	(2, 272)	0.0398**	0.0383**	0.1330	0.1310
Set 1b	00q3 + 06q2	(2, 272)	0.0381**	0.0366**	0.1251	0.1231
Set 2a	53q3 + 01q1	(2, 272	0.0283**	0.0270**	0.1333	0.1313
Set 2b	53q3 + 08q1	(2, 272)	0.0287**	0.0273**	0.1227	0.1207
Set 2c	53q2 + 07q4	(2, 272)	0.0209**	0.0198**	0.0966*	0.0947*
Set 2d	53q3 + 06q2	(2, 272)	0.0196**	0.0185**	0.0909*	0.0890*
Set 2e	53q2 + 00q3	(2, 272)	0.0172**	0.0162**	0.0912*	0.0893*
Set 2f	53q2 + 06q2	(2, 272)	0.0159**	0.0149**	0.0781*	0.0763*
Set 3a	73q2 + 00q3 + 06q2	(3. 271)	0.0438**	0.0417**	0.2039	0.2013
Set 4a	53q2 + 73q2 + 06q2	(3, 271)	0.0271**	0.0254**	0.1530	0.1502

The first number in parentheses before the comma gives the degrees of freedom associated with the Wald statistic *p*-value for the set in that row. Both numbers in parentheses show degrees of freedom for the *F*-test

Note that a single asterisk (*) denotes significance at the ten percent level, while two asterisks (**) denote significance at the five percent level

Set 1a has quarters 2000q3 and 2007q4. Set 1b has quarters 2000q3 and 2006q2

Set 2a has quarters 1953q3 and 2001q1. Set 2b has quarters 1953q3 and 2008q1

Set 2c has quarters 1953q2 and 2007q4. Set 2d has quarters 1953q3 and 2006q2

Set 2e has quarters 1953q2 and 2000q3. Set 2f has quarters 1953q2 and 2006q2

Set 3a has quarters 1973q2, 2000q3, and 2006q2

Set 4a has quarters 1953q2, 1973q2, and 2006q2

Sources www.economagic.com, Saint Louis Federal Reserve Bank FRED web page, U.S. Bureau of Economic Analysis, and the author's calculations

Unlike Model A discussed above, Model B with per capita data failed to find evidence of multiple breaks at or near the ten percent level among the initial five sets of recession-initiating quarters in Table 5.1 or those only in the appendix, with the closest to the ten percent level being Set 1 with *p*-values around the 16.6% level. However, some evidence of joint breaks in the intercept using alternate sets of quarters with Model B as shown in Table 5.2 found evidence of breaks at the ten percent level.

Among the ten alternate sets of quarters that I tried (with most alternate sets having at least one quarter that did not start a recession as defined in this book) where the results are in Table 5.2, four of those combinations found evidence of two breaks in the intercept of Model B at the ten percent level. Those sets are Set 2c (1953q2 and 2007q4), Set 2d (1953q3 and 2006q2), Set 2e (1953q2 and 2000q3) and Set 2f (1953q2 and 2006q2). When applied to Model A, all ten alternate sets found evidence of two or three joint breaks at the five percent level.

Note that the digit in the name of one of the alternate sets, for example the '1' in Set 1a or the '2' in Set 2f, represents a 'non-alternate' set that may be comparable to the alternate set in terms of the quarters selected. Thus, Set 1a may be comparable to Set 1, and Set 2f may be comparable to Set 2.

To recap quickly, the Chow (1960) breakpoint test found evidence of single breaks in many recession-starting quarters at the ten percent level for Model A with the change in the log of total U.S. real GDP. Some of those quarters also produced significance at the five percent level. Additionally, four alternate quarters soon before the start of a recession also produced evidence of a break at the five percent level, and one additional alternate quarter found evidence of a break at the 6.5% level. Model A also produced evidence of multiple breaks at the ten percent level if not the five percent level in many though not all cases.

Only two recession-starting quarters produced evidence of an intercept break when using Model B with the change in the log of per capita real GDP. That evidence was at the ten percent level and not the five percent level. Two alternate quarters produced evidence at the six percent level of a single intercept break using Model B. Four alternate sets with at least one quarter before the start of a recession as defined in this book produced evidence of two joint breaks in the intercept at the ten percent level in the per capita model. Does the fact that the Chow (1960) breakpoint test also found evidence (albeit at the ten percent level but not the five percent level) of breaks when using U.S. per capita real GDP suggest that not all breaks in the total real GDP series are due solely to changes in either the population or the population growth rate?

Before presenting results from other tests seeking evidence of breaks, readers may benefit from an example illustrating downward breaks in the intercept or constant of the Model A equation. Recall that Set 2 was the only set of the initial five that produced evidence of multiple breaks at the five percent level based on the F-statistic when using the Chow breakpoint test for Model A (Eq. 4.1). Set 2 consisted of the third quarter of 1953, the first quarter of 2001, and the first quarter of 2008.

Assuming three breaks, the intercept applicable to the period from the beginning of the sample period through the second quarter of 1953 was approximately 0.0083. Regression results imply that if a break occurred in the third quarter of 1953, then the estimated constant fell to about 0.00555. This is found by adding the estimated coefficient for the 1953q3 dummy variable, approximately −0.0027, to the estimated intercept, + 0.0083. The results also imply that if two additional breaks occurred in the first quarter of 2001 and the first quarter of 2008, then the estimated constant decreased to approximately 0.00395 from the first quarter of 2001 through the fourth quarter of 2007 and to approximately 0.00197 from the first quarter of 2008 through the second quarter of 2016, the end of the sample period. Again, adding the estimated coefficients for the dummy variables for breaks in the first quarters of 2001 and 2008, approximately −0.0016 and −0.0020, respectively, to the intercept that the model suggests was in place prior to each break, or about 0.00555 starting with 1953q3 but before 2001q1 and 0.00395 starting with 2001q1 but before 2008q1, generates the subsequent revised intercept terms.

To provide a sense of the potential impact of the decreases in the estimated constant on real output growth, the estimates imply that real output grew on average about 3.35% per year independent of the impact of the estimated slope coefficient times the changes in real output one quarter earlier (and independent of the residuals) through the second quarter of 1953. Beginning with the first break found in the third quarter of 1953, the intercept term contributed about 2.24% per year to real output growth, a decrease of more than one full percentage point. Starting with the second break found in the first quarter of 2001, the constant added only about 1.59% per year to annual real GDP growth. After the third break found by the Chow test, real output increased by only around 0.79% per year based on compounding the quarterly increase

Table 5.3 Regression results for Set 2 (with dummy variables for breaks in the third quarter of 1953, the first quarter of 2001, and the first quarter of 2008) using Model A (with the change in total real GDP)

Variable	*Coefficient*	*Stand. er*	t-*Stat*	p-*value*
C	0.008276	0.001911	4.329689	0.0000
DUM53	−0.002727	0.001907	−1.429883	0.1539
DUM01	−0.001597	0.001777	−0.898423	0.3698
DUM08	−0.001980	0.002241	−0.883570	0.3777
DLNY(−1)	0.335252	0.057034	5.878118	0.0000

The results can be used to calculate the non-constant intercept over different intervals
Sources www.economagic.com, Saint Louis Federal Reserve Bank, U.S. Bureau of Economic Analysis, and the author's calculations

given by the intercept (and ignoring the slope coefficient and the residuals) from the first quarter of 2008 through the second quarter of 2016. Additional evidence beyond the material in this chapter explaining at least one reason why it may be reasonable to think that decreases in aggregate demand could cause breaks in the trend growth path of real output in an economy appears in Chapter 6 in a section about derived demand and hysteresis.

Readers may want to note that evidence of breaks from Chow breakpoint testing when adding a time trend to the specifications of Eqs. 4.1 and 4.2 for Models A and B, respectively, may not be as strong as the results in this chapter. In part due to (a) lower Schwarz (1978) criteria results for Eqs. 4.1 and 4.2 without time trends and (b) possible questions about the statistical significance of the time trend when dummy variables are added to Eqs. 4.1 and 4.2, I do not consider further these cases in this book. Future work could analyze those results with trends and differenced data (Tables 5.3 and 5.4).

5.2 Wald Restriction Tests and *t*-Tests of Intercept Terms

Recall that we should not be overly confident in the results from the previous subsection due in part to possible violations of standard regression assumptions. Additionally, omitted variables and the possibility of Type I errors, the latter where the null hypothesis is rejected although it is true, also should give some caution. Perhaps we should use other testing

Table 5.4 The time-varying function determining the change in the natural log of total real GDP in the U.S. implied by the results for Set 2 in Table 5.1

Period	*Equation for the change in the log of total real GDP*
1947q3 through 1953q2	$DLNY_t = 0.008276 + 0.335252{*}DLNY_{t-1} + \varepsilon_t$
1953q3 through 2000q4	$DLNY_t = 0.005549 + 0.335252{*}DLNY_{t-1} + \varepsilon_t$
2001q1 through 2007q4	$DLNY_t = 0.003952 + 0.335252{*}DLNY_{t-1} + \varepsilon_t$
2008q1 through 2016q2	$DLNY_t = 0.001972 + 0.335252{*}DLNY_{t-1} + \varepsilon_t$

Sources www.economagic.com, Saint Louis Federal Reserve Bank, U.S. Bureau of Economic Analysis, and the author's calculations

methods to look for additional supporting evidence of the hypothesis that recessions, including those resulting from decreases in aggregate demand, can result in essentially permanent changes in the growth trajectory of the economy.

Recall violations of standard regression assumptions such as heteroskedasticity of residuals, serial correlation among the residuals, and residuals that are not normally distributed. Regarding these potential violations, results in the online appendix indicate that in many if not most or all cases, these violations seem either less of a problem or not a problem at all if the sample period is divided up into subsample periods. Most subsample periods span from the first quarter of decreasing U.S. real GDP in a recession as defined in this book through the last quarter of the subsequent expansion. However, such a division implies a substantial reduction in the number of quarters used to estimate each of the regressions. Related to that, could the weakened evidence for violations of standard regression assumptions when dividing the sample period simply be due to reduced abilities of the test statistics to conclude no violations of standard regression assumptions due to fewer observations? Or is it that dividing the sample period at the beginnings of recessions removes changes in the means and the variances in the time series variables?

Readers may also want to remember that the Wald results from Chow (1960) breakpoint tests in the previous subsection may be asymptotically valid despite residuals that may fail to follow the standard assumptions. The greater likelihood of adherence to standard regression assumptions may be more important for the variation of the t-test to be discussed after the Wald restriction test, the latter of which is likely to be asymptotically valid.

The online appendix has regression results for dividing the sample period into ten subsample periods largely as described above. One exception is that the first quarter of the first subsample period is the first quarter of 1947, the beginning of the availability of quarterly data, well after the start of a recession that began based on annual data in 1945, according to data compiled by the U.S. Bureau of Economic Analysis (2017) and accessed from the FRED web page of the Saint Louis Federal Reserve Bank. (Readers may want to note that fitted or predicted values for the regressions for the first subsample period and for the differenced-data regressions for the full sample period start with the third quarter of 1947. One quarterly observation is lost due to differencing the data, while another quarter is lost due to the use of one lagged value of the change in real GDP.) Another exception is that the last subsample period ends with the second quarter of 2016 based on data availability as work on this book was in progress.

The approach in this section is to look for substantial decreases in the estimated intercepts of equations for the change in the natural log of either total U.S. real GDP or per capita U.S. real GDP between two consecutive subsample periods and then to perform Wald restriction tests and t-tests with the intercepts or constants to determine whether a statistically significant decrease in the estimated intercept occurred. I will focus on results from tests between (a) the first two subsample periods and (b) the last two subsample periods. Most of the discussion of the t-test results for intercepts between subsample periods will be only in the online appendix.

The table in the appendix shows that the estimated constant in Model A from the first subsample period, running from 1947 through the second quarter of 1953, is approximately 0.0082, and the estimated constant for the second subsample period, spanning from the third quarter of 1953 through the fourth quarter of 1955, is approximately 0.0018. These two estimated intercepts, 0.0082 and 0.0018, are analogous to C_A in Eq. 4.1, but C_A in that equation is at least implicitly estimated over the full sample period. Recall that the third quarter of 1953 was the start of a negative-aggregate-demand-shock recession.

Does the Wald restriction test find evidence of a difference in these two estimated constants? When testing that the estimated constant in the first subsample period, roughly 0.0082, is actually equal to the estimated value in the second period, roughly 0.0018, the Wald test Chi-squared statistic finds evidence of a difference not at the five percent level but at the ten percent level and the 7.5% level. The same is true when testing that the value of the estimated constant in the second subsample period actually equals its estimated value from the first subsample period, roughly 0.0082, although we may possibly want to emphasize the results from the test for the second subsample period intercept in the first subsample period regression due to a larger number of observations in the first subsample period. Readers can see the results in Table 5.5.

A negative AD shock also separated the ninth and tenth subsample periods. A relatively large decrease in the estimated intercept occurred between the two periods. The Wald coefficient restriction test using the Chi-squared distribution rejects the null hypothesis at the five percent level (and rather close to the four percent level) that the estimated coefficient in the ninth subsample period of approximately 0.0046 is actually about 0.0017, which was approximately the estimated value from the last subsample period, running the test based on the regression in the ninth subsample period. The estimated constants, analogous to C_A from the full sample regression Eq. (4.1), are from a table in the appendix. As shown in Table 5.5, the *p*-value for the test statistic was approximately 0.041. Realizing that the estimated constants in the regressions are likely at least asymptotically consistent even if they may be biased, the findings offer statistical support for the view that the constant decreased from the ninth subsample period to the tenth subsample period.

When testing that the estimated constant from the tenth subsample period is actually equal to its value from the ninth period using the

Table 5.5 Wald Coefficient Restriction test *p*-values for Chi-squared statistics

	47q3-53q2/ 53q3-55q4 Constant from later period	*Constant from earlier period*	*01q1-07q4/ 08q1-16q2 Constant from later period*	*Constant from earlier period*
Model A	0.0725*	0.0717*	0.0411**	0.0146**
Model B	0.1143	0.1323	0.0469**	0.0501*

Note that (1) 'Constant from Later Period' in a column means testing the estimated intercept from the later subsample period in the earlier regression and 'Constant from Earlier Period' means testing the constant from the earlier subsample period in the later regression, and (2) a single asterisk (*) denotes significance at the ten percent level, while two asterisks (**) denote significance at the five percent level

Sources www.economagic.com, Saint Louis Federal Reserve Bank FRED web page, U.S. Bureau of Economic Analysis, and the author's calculations

regression in the tenth subsample period, the Wald test rejects the null hypothesis at the five percent level, with a *p*-value of approximately 0.015. Readers should note that the regression residuals from the tenth subsample period are almost certainly not normally distributed. More about possible violations of standard regression assumptions for the subsample periods appears in the appendix.

Table 5.5 also has *p*-values associated with Chi-squared statistics for Wald restriction tests using Model B with the change in the natural log of per capita U.S. real GDP for the same subsample periods as those in the table displaying results for Model A. A table in the appendix shows that the estimated intercepts for Model B (comparable to C_B in Eq. 4.2) from the first two subsample periods, are approximately 0.00534 and 0.00052, respectively, with the estimated intercept in the second subsample period approximately one-tenth of its value from the first subsample period. Results in Table 5.5 show evidence of an intercept break somewhat close to, but not quite at the ten percent level. Testing the intercept from the second subsample period in the regression for the first subsample period has a *p*-value a bit less than 0.115. When testing the estimated constant from the first subsample period in the second subsample period regression, the *p*-value is about 0.132.

Testing the intercepts from the ninth and tenth subsample periods from Model B produced stronger evidence of an intercept break between those two subsample periods, as was the case with Model A. As shown in the appendix, the estimated constant from the ninth subsample period was roughly 0.00273 and fell to about 0.00056 in the tenth subsample period. Testing the estimated constant from the tenth subsample period in the regression for the ninth subsample period found evidence of a difference at the five percent level. When instead testing the estimated intercept from the ninth subsample period in the regression equation for the tenth subsample period, the *p*-value was slightly above the five percent level.

To sum up briefly, evidence of two breaks between two combinations of subsample periods, (a) the first and the second subsample periods, and (b) the ninth and the tenth subsample periods exists at the 13.5% level or better for both Model A and Model B. Between the ninth and tenth subsample periods, both models found evidence of a difference in the intercepts at the 5.1% level or better regardless of whether the estimated intercept from the later subsample period was tested in the earlier regression or whether the estimated intercept from the earlier subsample period was tested in the later regression. Between the first and second subsample periods, the evidence for a difference in intercepts was found at the 7.5% level in Model A and between the 11.0 and the 13.5% levels in Model B depending on which of the intercepts was tested in which regression equation. Recessions that appear to have been induced by decreases in aggregate demand led to the start of the second and the tenth subsample periods.

The Wald restriction tests above and the *t*-statistic tests referenced below and listed in the appendix focus on cases where the start of a new subsample period resulted in a notable decrease in the estimated intercepts of Models A and B. Readers should realize that, as shown in the appendix, the estimated intercept sometimes increased between consecutive subsample periods, although those cases were not presented in the table above.

Given violations of standard regression assumptions, many if not most or all of the tests for breaks presented to this point are technically valid only asymptotically and not within a finite sample period. The appendix has results from *t*-statistic tests for (a) the first and second subsample periods and (b) the ninth and tenth subsample periods that may be valid within a finite sample period. Some of these tests in the appendix may be valid due to adherence to standard regression assumptions in regressions over subsample periods (rather than over the full sample period). Other tests may be valid due to adjustments in light of possible heteroskedasticity and/or serial correlation. The *t*-statistic tests question whether the intercept from one subsample period equals the estimated value from another subsample period either immediately before or immediately after rather than testing whether the true value of the estimated intercept is zero.

The *t*-test results indicate possible evidence of one or two downward breaks in the intercepts of Model A and Model B equations between subsample periods separated by a negative-AD-shock induced recession. The evidence of downward breaks in the intercepts associated with negative AD shocks was either at or somewhat near the ten percent level in a one-sided test in all cases and at the five percent level or better in two-sided tests in some cases. Without corrections for possible violations of standard regression assumptions, all eight *t*-statistic tests found evidence of a change in the intercept between subsample periods at the ten percent level or better. With corrections, the tests still found evidence of a change at the ten percent level in seven of the eight cases, with the lone exception somewhat close to the ten percent level.

Clearly, such corrections for heteroskedasticity and serial correlation are not the area of my greatest expertise, and so the results should be received with appropriate caution. However, given the encouraging nature of the results and their potential importance, I decided to include them in the online appendix.

5.3 Chow Forecast Test Results

We have discussed possible evidence of structural breaks in the first differences of the natural logs of real output and per capita real output occurring at or near the onsets of some if not many recessions based on Chow breakpoint testing, the Wald restriction test, and the *t*-test. Results differ dramatically when using the Chow forecast test. EViews 10 offers the Chow forecast test where users can test for a break in one time period in a trial.

With the Chow forecast test, of the trials that I have conducted, not one trial from Model A or Model B produces evidence of a change at the five percent level, the ten percent level, or any level even remotely close! I wanted to mention this finding here to present a fuller picture. However, I will place most of the statistical findings from the Chow forecast tests only in the appendix of this chapter in part due to the relative monotony of the findings.

To give an example about the high degree of sameness in the results and how little evidence of breaks exists when using the Chow forecast test, of the results from the two models using differenced data, the smallest *p*-value for any trial of the Chow forecast test of the quarters that I tried occurred in the first quarter of 2008 in Model A. EViews reported a *p*-value for that test of 0.9597. That is quite a bit above the ten-percent *p*-value of 0.10 and in fact getting close to the maximum *p*-value of 1.0. I include the Chow forecast test results briefly here but mainly in the online appendix to show that not all evidence suggests that breaks or changes in the data-generating process have occurred, at least with or near the onsets of recessions. I think that the results presented to this point and those to follow in this book suggest that the topic merits further study and attention.

Note that the Chow forecast tests are for breaks in all of the regressors (or right-side variables) in the regression equation, not only the constant. Also in the table in the appendix showing Chow forecast test results are *p*-values from Chow breakpoint tests of all regressors rather than just the constants. The Chow breakpoint results in the appendix are provided mainly for comparison purposes. Readers may want to note that the EViews 10 User's Guide II (2017, p. 223) notes, in the context of an example different from the cases that are the focus of this chapter (and book), the Chow breakpoint test and the Chow forecast test could yield very different results with the Chow breakpoint test rejecting the null hypothesis of no break but the Chow forecast test failing to reject.

Readers should also realize that other methods exist to test for breaks. If it is valid (a) to use un-differenced data and (b) to test for breaks in at least one term that may not be statistically significant, then tentative preliminary results from my use of one other method suggest that one or two breaks in the intercept and/or trend from the equations for Model A and Model B may have occurred. Further work on this could occur in the future.

5.4 Testing for a Unit Root with a Break: Tentative Results

False conclusions present a possible concern with unmodified unit root tests in the presence of a break in the series, according to the EViews 10 User's Guide II (2017, p. 602), perhaps based on Perron (1989). For example, a variable could be in essence a trend stationary variable (stationary but for a trend) except for one break that causes a standard unit root test to conclude perhaps incorrectly that the variable has a unit root. The one break could cause a unit root test to fail to reject the null hypothesis of a unit root when the test perhaps ideally would reject the hypothesis if only one shock to the variable had an impact that did not fade away. More about the possible benefits of using multiple hypothesis tests follows.

One of the potential drawbacks of the tests for breaks (for example, the Chow breakpoint tests and the Wald restriction tests) using the natural logs of total U.S. real GDP and per capita U.S. real GDP only in differenced form on both sides of the regression equations is that it is not possible, at least to my knowledge, to test for a break in the intercept of the equation specification using the variable in level or log level form because (1) the intercept in the equation for the change in the log level of the variable corresponds with or is analogous to the trend coefficient for the equation in log level form and (2) differencing the data implies that the intercept of the equation in (log) level form disappears through subtraction.

For example, consider a simple trend line for a variable Y in time period t with an intercept (I) greater than zero in Eq. 5.1.

$$Y_t = I + 3 * t \tag{5.1}$$

One period earlier, in period $t-1$, the equation for variable Y in time period $t-1$ is given by Eq. 5.2.

$$Y_{t-1} = I + 3 * (t - 1) \tag{5.2}$$

Differencing the data for the change in variable Y in time period t, we find in Eq. 5.3.

$$Y_t - Y_{t-1} = I + 3 * t - [I + 3 * (t - 1)] = 3 \tag{5.3}$$

Note that 3 is the trend coefficient.

Readers should note that I am uncertain about how applicable the algebraic analysis above is for this chapter due to the lack of any lagged values of Y, a lack of an error term in Eqs. (5.1) and (5.2), and a change in scale. But to the extent that it applies, it helps to make a point. Notice that the intercept I disappears from the trend equation in differenced form. Those interested can verify that for a small, imaginary economy with Y representing annual real data (not necessarily in natural log form), (a) if the intercept equals 2 and the year t is 2000, then Yt equals 6002, (b) if the intercept equals 2 but the year is one year earlier (1999), then Yt equals 5999, and (c) the change in Yt in the year 2000 equals 3.

By contrast, breakpoint unit root testing with data both on the left side of the regression equation and also at least one term on the right side of the equation in (log) level form permits a break in the intercept (or the trend or both the intercept and trend) in the regression equation in (log) level form, although the breakpoint unit root test regression equations obviously will not be exactly the same as the regression equations above for changes in the logs of total and per capita real GDP (in Chow breakpoint testing, etc.) or the corresponding regression equations in (log) level form. An obvious difference would be that the breakpoint unit root test regression equations have data in both un-differenced form and in differenced form (or data with fewer differencing operations and more differencing operations, for example data in first difference form and second difference form), while the Chow breakpoint testing equations in Sect. 5.1 have all output variables in 'change in the log of' form.

A possible advantage of the breakpoint tests with differenced data in this book such as the Chow breakpoint tests, to the extent that they are valid, is that the tests permit breaks in the intercept in differenced form which *may* be similar to breaks in the trend coefficient in log level form. Additional possible advantages of other breakpoint testing methods compared with breakpoint unit root testing are that (1) breakpoint unit root testing may not be intended as a test for breaks, (2) it is easy to test for breaks in two or more quarters in the same trial in Chow breakpoint testing but either more difficult or impossible in breakpoint unit root testing, and (3) with short lag structures (two lags in log level form, one lag in first difference of log form), it is possible when dividing up the sample period into subsample periods (most spanning a business cycle from the start of a recession through the end of the next expansion) to have a sufficient number of data observations to test for a change in the intercept with the equation in first difference of log level form for the recessions that started in the first quarter of 1949 (although few if any of the tests in this chapter sought a break in that quarter) and the first quarter of 1956.

Readers may recall that not many lags of data are needed to use the Chow forecast test. However, given that real GDP returned to pre-recession trend following the recession in 1949 using the Chapter 3 methodology, it does not seem necessary to use the Chow forecast test to test for a break at some point in the year 1949. In many of the trials of the breakpoint unit root tests in this book, the F-statistic and t-statistic methods select twelve lags of the change in the log of the output variable in the test regression equations (although I could have chosen the Schwarz [1978] criterion method, which likely would have selected fewer lagged first differences).

Thus, with the quarterly data sample period starting with the first quarter of 1947, fewer than three years of data preclude testing for a break in the first quarter of 1949 if a larger number of lags is needed. When dividing the sample period as discussed above, given that a recession started in the third quarter of 1953 and another started in the first quarter of 1956, only ten quarters of data are in the subsample period spanning from the third quarter of 1953 through the fourth quarter of 1955. In some other cases, there would only be a few more than twelve quarters, such as the fourth quarter of 1969 through the second quarter of 1973. The parsimonious lag structure used earlier in the chapter based on minimizing the Schwarz criterion (with a maximum of five lags) easily provides sufficient observations for dividing the sample period in the way discussed. Given the advantages and disadvantages, perhaps it is better to consider results from all of the methods used in this chapter rather than to rely on one method only.

The main focus of this book is not whether the two real output series have unit roots or whether these two series are better modeled as trend stationary but with at least one break in each series. Rather, one of the critical issues is whether recessions, including those caused by decreases in aggregate demand, can lead to permanent or essentially permanent changes in the growth paths of total real GDP and per capita real GDP, and if so, why that may be true. For example, could rising economic inequality have led to downward breaks in the trend growth path of real GDP in the U.S.? If real output has a unit root, then that has clear implications for the impacts of recessions. This is a point made by Hamilton (1994, p. 444). However, even if real output does not have a unit root but is trend stationary but with one or more breaks associated with recessions, then recessions could still permanently impact future realizations of the real GDP variable.

Unfortunately, I cannot offer definitive answers with this book. In this book, I would like to raise questions about statistical properties of real output and the way that many think about recessions. Toward the end of this book and in my next book (hint, hint), I would like to begin to address how economic inequality and other factors could be associated with recessions and general reductions in economic growth. Clearly, this book is part of a 'beginning' rather than an 'end.' As a part of that 'beginning,' please allow me to offer the econometric tests above, to the extent that they are valid, for breaks in the intercepts for the equations with the first differences of the natural logs of either total U.S. real GDP or per capita U.S. real GDP on the left sides of the test regression equations as *possible* evidence of changes in the trend coefficients for the versions of the models with the un-differenced log levels on the left sides of the regression equations. Also, please allow me to offer both breakpoint unit root tests in this section and augmented Dickey–Fuller (1979)(ADF) unit root tests mentioned in an earlier section as evidence of the possible permanence of the impacts of some shocks. Given that (1) I am not in the area of my greatest expertise and (2) I would like to make the findings available as soon as possible, I will leave improvements, revisions, and corrections for future work.

In working on this book, I have conducted breakpoint unit root tests differing in terms of whether I specified the breaking quarter or whether I allowed the software to select it based on minimizing the ADF statistic and thus maximizing the likelihood of rejecting the null hypothesis of a unit root (when searching for a break in quarters throughout the sample period). In some test trials, I have chosen the quarter that started a recession to be the breaking quarter, and in other cases a different quarter. Further, in some cases, I have chosen to use the F-statistic method for selecting the number of lagged first differences of the log of the output variable to include, and in other cases I have used the t-statistic method. Moreover, some of the tests end the sample period before the second quarter of 2016. Although the test trials have these differences, I believe that with the possible exception of the appendix, I present results from breakpoint unit root testing only for trials of the test (a) allowing a break only in the intercept with the dependent variable in log level form and (b) with the sample period spanning through either the second quarter of 2016 (to be presented shortly) or through the fourth quarter 2019 (in Chapter 7). In light of the facts that I am a newcomer to breakpoint unit root testing and that I am striving for readability, I will only briefly discuss breakpoint unit root test results here and place most of the results and discussion in the appendix for this chapter.

When I allow (1) the ADF statistic procedure to select the breaking quarter and (2) the F-statistic approach to select the number of lagged first differences of the log of output, I fail to reject the null hypothesis of a unit root when using the log of quarterly U.S. real GDP data from the first quarter of 1947 through the second quarter of 2016. In fact, the p-value associated with the test statistic is greater than 0.860. The breaking quarter selected by minimizing the ADF statistic was the fourth quarter of 2007, just one quarter before the start of the Great Recession. My understanding of the EViews 10 User's Guide II (2017, p. 607) is that selecting the breaking quarter in this way makes it most likely *within this test trial* to reject the null hypothesis of a unit root.

However, if I specify the fourth quarter of 2007 as the breaking quarter, then despite producing the same test statistic, the test rejects the null hypothesis of a unit root with a break at the ten percent level but not at the five percent level. (Note that evidently, whether the break date is either predetermined or selected based on minimizing the ADF statistic can have an impact on the p-values and thus the conclusions of the test.) I find qualitatively similar results as the results from specifying the fourth quarter of 2007 as the breaking quarter when specifying instead the first quarter of 2008, the first quarter of falling real output data in the Great Recession, as the breaking quarter. Using the first quarter of 2008 as the breaking quarter could improve the comparability with some of the Chow breakpoint test results discussed earlier. In all three breakpoint unit root test cases for the log of total U.S. real GDP in Table 5.6, the dummy variable for a downward intercept break is statistically significant (assuming that any possible violations of standard regression assumptions or other possible issues do not create a problem for such statistical inference).

Table 5.6 displays breakpoint unit root test results over the full sample period (through the second quarter of 2016) for the log of total U.S. real GDP. In addition to a dummy variable for a permanent break indicated by the word 'Intercept' in the table, the software also has a dummy variable for a temporary one period break in the test regression. This is indicated by '1-Time' in Table 5.6.

According to the EViews 10 User's Guide II (2017, pp. 610–614), Perron (1997) found an intercept break in the annual U.S. real GNP

Table 5.6 Selected breakpoint unit root test results for the natural log of total U.S. real GDP

End quarter	*Break quarter*	*ADF stat*	*Stat p-value*	*Dummy type*	*Dummy coefficient*	*Dummy p-value*
2016q2	2007q4	−3.152243	0.8620	Intercept	−0.010316	0.0004
				One-time	0.004765	0.5724
2016q2	2007q4#	−3.152243	<0.10	Intercept	−0.010316	0.0004
				One-time	0.004765	0.5724
2016q2	2008q1#	−2.972565	<0.10	Intercept	−0.009782	0.0010
				One-time	−0.003966	0.6386

Intercept refers to an intercept dummy variable (for a permanent change in the intercept) starting in the breaking quarter, One-Time refers to a dummy variable for a temporary one-quarter change in the intercept in the breaking quarter. Both the F-statistic approach and the t-statistic approach selected twelve lagged first differences of the log of total U.S. real GDP for the test equation

Note # denotes the author's selection of the break date. Approximate critical values for these cases where the author selected the break date—five percent: −3.4, ten percent: −2.4

Sources www.economagic.com, Saint Louis Federal Reserve Bank, U.S. Bureau of Economic Analysis, EViews 10, Vogelsang (1993), Perron (1989), Perron and Vogelsang (1993), and the author's calculations

series in 1929, prior to the start of the sample period that I use. (Technically, the EViews 10 User's Guide II (2017, p. 612) states that Perron (1997) reported 1928 as the breaking year, the last year with the old intercept rather than 1929, the year starting the new intercept.) I have found either an intercept break in the fourth quarter of 2007 (or the first quarter of 2008) or a unit root process for quarterly real GDP (or perhaps two or more breaks). Regardless, it looks like at least some AD shocks can have either a permanent or an essentially permanent impact on real output! For more, readers can see the appendix.

The use of per capita U.S. real GDP data produces largely similar results. When allowing the software to find the potentially breaking quarter based on minimizing the ADF statistic, again I fail to reject the null hypothesis of a unit root in the log of the per capita U.S. real GDP series, with a *p*-value associated with the test statistic of roughly 0.69. The breaking quarter selected based on the ADF statistic was the fourth quarter of 2007. However, if I specify the fourth quarter of 2007 as the breaking quarter, then I reject the null hypothesis of a unit root in the U.S. per capita real output series at the five percent level in favor of the alternate hypothesis that the per capita U.S. real GDP series is trend stationary but with an intercept break. Alternatively, if I specify the first quarter of 2008 as the breaking quarter, then I reject the null hypothesis of a unit root, however not at the five percent level but rather at the ten percent level. Table 5.7 has the breakpoint unit root test results with data for the log of per capita U.S. real GDP through the second quarter of 2016.

Readers can refer to sources such as Vogelsang and Perron (1998) and the EViews 10 User's Guide II (2017, pp. 604–606) for information about which cases in breakpoint unit root testing allow a break in the trend coefficient under the null hypothesis of a unit root. Future breakpoint unit root testing work could analyze the impact of allowing a break in both the intercept and the trend coefficient.

In light of (1) unit root test results in the appendix that clearly fail to reject the null hypothesis of a unit root in the natural logs of the two real output series, (2) the breakpoint unit root test results immediately above, and (3) results from Chow breakpoint testing, the Wald restriction tests, and the *t*-statistic tests earlier in the chapter and in the online appendix, I tentatively conclude that the natural logs of U.S. total real GDP and U.S. per capita real GDP are better considered as either true unit root processes or trend stationary but with at least one break where a negative AD shock

Table 5.7 Selected breakpoint unit root test results for the natural log of per capita U.S. real GDP

End quarter	*Break quarter*	*ADF stat*	*Stat* p-*value*	*Dummy type*	*Dummy coefficient*	*Dummy* p-*value*
2016q2	2007q4	−3.501445	0.6913	Intercept	−0.010959	0.0002
				One-Time	0.005337	0.5280
2016q2	2007q4#	−3.501445	<0.05	Intercept	−0.010959	0.0002
				One-Time	0.005337	0.5280
2016q2	2008q1#	−3.327502	<0.10	Intercept	−0.010531	0.0004
				One-Time	−0.002789	0.7419

Intercept refers to an intercept dummy variable (for a permanent change in the intercept) starting in the breaking quarter, 1-Time refers to a dummy variable for a temporary one-quarter change in the intercept in the breaking quarter. Both the F-statistic approach and the t-statistic approach selected twelve lagged first differences of the log of per capita U.S. real GDP for the test equation

Note # denotes the author's selection of the break date. Approximate critical values for these cases where the author selected the break date—five percent: −3.4, ten percent: −2.4

Sources Saint Louis Federal Reserve Bank FRED web page, U.S. Bureau of Economic Analysis, EViews 10, Vogelsang (1993), Perron (1989), Perron and Vogelsang (1993), and the author's calculations

could have caused the break. Future work could try to determine which of those two possibilities better characterizes each or both of those two time series variables. My interpretation of the possibility that the real output variables may have unit roots allows at least some AD shocks to have permanent impacts on real GDP.

It may be worth remembering that the Chow forecast test trials that I have conducted found no evidence of any breaks. Future work could also analyze results from other tests for multiple breaks using the method or methods of Bai (1997) and Bai and Perron (1998, 2003a, 2003b) and others.

Given the possibility of multiple breaks, the appendix has breakpoint unit root tests where the sample period stops before the fourth quarter of 2007. If it is valid to divide up the sample period when conducting breakpoint unit root testing to search for more than one break over the full sample period, then readers may want to note that a tentative conclusion is that a possible *upward* intercept break occurred in the mid-1960s, around the time of expansionary fiscal policy.

Regarding key takeaways from breakpoint unit root testing in this section and unit root testing in the appendix, note that none of the tests concluded that the natural logs of total U.S. real GDP and per capita

U.S. real GDP were trend stationary *without any breaks*. Results in the appendix for traditional unit root testing find that these variables have unit roots. Some of the breakpoint unit root tests in the body of the chapter also conclude that these variables have unit roots *despite allowing for a single intercept break under the alternate hypothesis*, while others reject at the ten percent level (and in one case at the five percent level) the null hypothesis of a unit root in favor of the alternate hypothesis of trend stationarity but with an intercept break around the start of the Great Recession. In all six cases of breakpoint unit root testing in the body of the chapter, the dummy variable for a permanent downward shift in either the fourth quarter of 2007 or the first quarter of 2008 was statistically significant to the extent that the results are valid. Regardless of whether U.S. real output is truly a unit root process or trend stationary with at least one break, this seems to suggest that decreases in aggregate demand can potentially have long-term negative consequences for real GDP. Further, it appears that given similar results in many cases for U.S. per capita real output, not all of the possible breaks found for total U.S. real GDP can be explained solely by changes in either population or the population growth rate.

5.5 Brief Summary of Results from Testing for Breaks

This chapter presented results from approaches testing for breaks in the natural logs of U.S. total real GDP and U.S. per capita real GDP. Many of the results from Chow (1960) breakpoint testing, Wald coefficient restriction testing, *t*-statistic testing (most of which appears only in the online appendix), and breakpoint unit root testing supported the view that decreases in aggregate demand matter beyond the short term, if not permanently, with results perhaps using total real GDP more supportive than using per capita real GDP. Results from Chow forecast tests failed to find support for the hypothesis of any breaks.

If one takes the view that downward breaks in the log of total U.S. real GDP have occurred, then one would probably like to understand why. The next chapter, Chapter 6, begins to analyze how employment may be a factor.

References

Bai, J. (1997). Estimating multiple breaks one at a time. *Econometric Theory, 13*, 315–352.

Bai, J., & Perron, P. (1998). Estimating and testing linear models with multiple structural changes. *Econometrica, 66*, 47–78.

Bai, J., & Perron, P. (2003a). Computation and analysis of multiple structural change models. *Journal of Applied Econometrics, 6*, 72–78.

Bai, J., & Perron, P. (2003b). Critical values for multiple structural change tests. *Econometrics Journal, 18*, 1–22.

Chow, G. C. (1960). Tests of equality between sets of coefficients in two linear regressions. *Econometrica, 28*(3), 591–605.

Dickey, D. A., & Fuller, W. A. (1979). Distribution of the estimators for autoregressive time series with a unit root. *Journal of the American Statistical Association, 74*, 427–431.

EViews 10 User's Guide II. (2017). IHS Global, Inc. Irvine, CA.

Hamilton, J. D. (1994). *Time series analysis*. Princeton University Press.

Perron, P. (1989). The great crash, the oil price shock, and the unit root hypothesis. *Econometrica, 57*, 1361–1401.

Perron, P. (1997). Further evidence on breaking trend functions in macroeconomic variables. *Journal of Econometrics, 80*, 355–385.

Perron, P., & Vogelsang, T. J. (1993). Nonstationarity and level shifts with an application to purchasing power parity. *Journal of Business and Economics Statistics, 10*, 301–320.

Schwarz, G. (1978). Estimating the dimension of a model. *Annals of Statistics, 6*, 461–464.

Vogelsang, T. J. (1993). *Computer program* (unpublished).

Vogelsang, T. J., & Pierre, P. (1998). Additional tests for a unit root allowing for a break in the trend function at an unknown time. *International Economic Review, 39*(4), 1073–1100. *JSTOR*. www.jstor.org/stable/2527353. https://doi.org/10.2307/2527353

U.S. Bureau of Economic Analysis. (2016, November 2). *Real gross domestic product per capita [A939RX0Q048SBEA]*. Retrieved from FRED, Federal Reserve Bank of St. Louis. https://fred.stlouisfed.org/series/A939RX0Q048SBEA

U.S. Bureau of Economic Analysis. (2017, August 9). *Real Gross Domestic Product [GDPCA]*. Retrieved from FRED, Federal Reserve Bank of St. Louis; https://fred.stlouisfed.org/series/GDPCA. But The Data Were Probably Accessed August 9, 2017 (although the web page stated August 8, 2017)

www.economagic.com

CHAPTER 6

Derived Demand for Labor and Breaks in Trend: Does Hysteresis in Employment Imply Hysteresis in the Growth Path of Real Output?

Abstract With earlier chapters finding evidence supporting the view that at least some decreases in aggregate demand have resulted in downward breaks in U.S. real GDP, this chapter begins seeking explanations by investigating whether decreases in AD have also led to downward breaks in U.S. employment. Using the natural log of total nonfarm payroll employment in the U.S. as the measure of employment, this chapter finds evidence of one or two breaks in U.S. nonfarm payroll employment in the intercept of an equation for the change in the log of U.S. nonfarm payroll employment based on Chow (1960) breakpoint testing. Could this suggest breaks in the trend coefficient for a similar regression equation with the data in log level form rather than change in the log form? The downward breaks in employment occurred around the times of AD shock recessions in 1953 and 2001. Also, if the testing is valid, breakpoint unit root testing finds a break in the intercept of an equation for U.S. nonfarm payroll employment in log level form around the start of the Great Recession. Less employment implies at least some will have less spending power. Additionally, do recessions sometimes cause decreases in population growth?

H. C. Hartman, *Bad Breaks in Real GDP and Employment*, https://doi.org/10.1007/978-3-031-57769-7_6

Keywords Employment · Unemployment · Breakpoint unit root testing · Chow breakpoint testing · Aggregate demand · Real GDP · Hysteresis · Macroeconomics

6.1 The Demand for Labor and a Very Brief Description of U.S. Nonfarm Payroll Employment—A Nonstationary Series

An old economic concept comes to mind that may help us to understand better the relatively sluggish growth in wages and salaries in the U.S., particularly slow in nominal terms given relatively rapid money supply growth after the year 2007. The idea is that the demand for labor is a form of derived demand. Profit-seeking employers demand the labor services of employees primarily if not exclusively because they anticipate that customers will be willing and able to purchase the goods and/or services that firms produce at least in part using the labor services of the firms' employees. Therefore, relatively weak growth in compensation could be at least partly due to relatively weak growth in aggregate demand.

If anyone needs convincing that growth in aggregate demand has been relatively weak following the Great Recession, then remember that the M1 money supply in the U.S. has more than quadrupled since the end of 2007. The increase in nominal GDP spending, however, serving as a measure of the change in aggregate demand by capturing the change in real GDP spending and the change in the price level, has increased by a much smaller percentage. Could it be that wage and salary growth would have been much greater had aggregate demand growth been greater? In turn, would aggregate demand growth have been stronger if wealth inequality and income inequality had not increased so dramatically?

Much of the previous chapter sought evidence as to whether recessions, including those associated with negative aggregate demand shocks, were also associated with downward breaks in the trend growth paths of the natural logs of real GDP and per capita real GDP, both in the U.S. The evidence presented supporting this view suggests that recessions can be costly to an economy because the economy may not fully make up for the real output lost during recessions in subsequent recoveries. Could downward breaks in employment occurring at or near the times of recessions also have occurred? If so, then such downward breaks in employment would support the hypothesis that recessions led to downward breaks in the growth path of real GDP in the U.S. unless increases or improvements in factors such as technology, productivity, and/or the stock of physical capital or other non-labor resources and/or an increase in aggregate demand would have been sufficient to offset the negative effects of the recession causing employment in the U.S. to have failed to return to its former growth path.

Using the U3 unemployment rate alone may not be sufficient to judge the health of the labor market in an economy. Factors such as unplanned early retirements and longer term increases in the number of discouraged workers who do not seek employment due to the perceived low(er) probability of finding a job could result from weaker performance of the labor market but do not show up in the U3 unemployment rate. People who would prefer full-time employment but can find part-time work only also do not appear in U3. These effects do appear in a broader measure of the unemployment rate such as U6.

I used seasonally adjusted, monthly data from the FRED web page of the Saint Louis Federal Reserve and compiled by the U.S. Bureau of Labor Statistics (2020) for total U.S. nonfarm payroll employment in thousands. The data were accessed on May 16, 2020.

Figure 6.1 shows the natural log of nonfarm payroll employment in the U.S., both private and government, from January 1939 through December 2017. Notice that the graph may appear somewhat similar to the graphs of the natural logs of U.S. total real GDP and U.S. per capita real GDP from earlier chapters. The real output graphs from earlier chapters and the payroll employment graph depict variables that tend to increase over time. However, the graphs for both the real output variables and the payroll employment variable do not necessarily show variables oscillating around an unchanging trend line. Is there statistically significant evidence for at least one break in the trend of the log of estimated total U.S. nonfarm payroll employment?

Phillips–Perron (1988) (PP) unit root tests in the appendix fail to reject at the five percent level the null hypothesis that the natural logarithm of total U.S. nonfarm payroll employment has a unit root under different sets of assumptions about an intercept and/or a trend in the test regression equation. However, one case (of three) would reject the

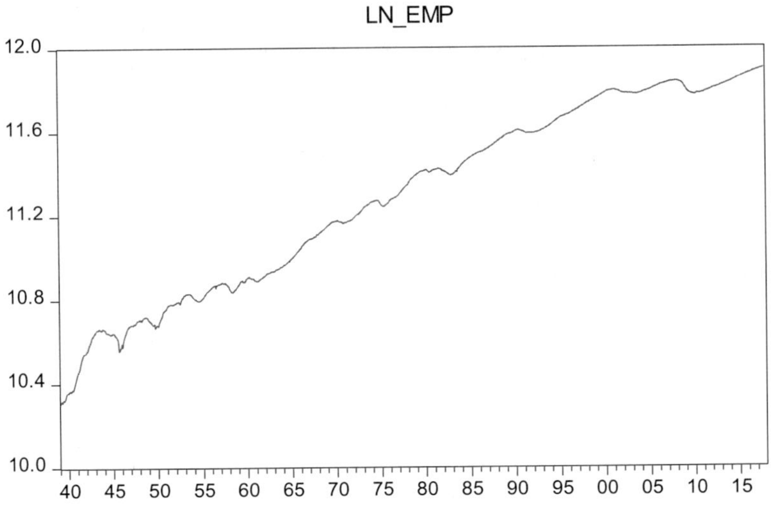

Fig. 6.1 The natural log of monthly U.S. nonfarm payroll employment (in thousands), January 1939 through December 2017 (*Sources* U.S. Bureau of Labor Statistics, Saint Louis Federal Reserve Bank FRED web page, and the author's calculations)

null hypothesis at the six percent level. Augmented Dickey–Fuller (1979) unit root tests, largely suppressed both here and in the appendix due to concerns about residuals that may not be consistent with standard regression assumptions, fail to reject the null hypothesis of a unit root in the log of total nonfarm payroll employment at either the five percent level or the ten percent level, although in two of three cases the rejection would be somewhat close to the ten percent level. If breakpoint unit root testing and Chow breakpoint testing find evidence of breaks, then I will assume that most likely the log of total U.S. nonfarm payroll employment is either (a) trend stationary but with at least one break or (b) a true unit root process, either of which would explain the failure to reject the unit root null hypothesis at the five percent level.

As was the question or the issue with the two real output series in the previous chapter, could just one break be responsible for the nonstationary finding for the log of the nonfarm payroll employment series, or is the finding due to the log of the payroll employment series being either a true unit root process or a trend stationary process but with at least two breaks? Just as this book could not offer a definitive answer about whether the natural logs of the per capita real output series and the total real output series in the U.S. were better considered as unit root processes or trend stationary but with one or more breaks in the trend of each series, this book cannot offer a firm conclusion about whether the natural log of total U.S. nonfarm payroll employment would be better categorized as having a unit root or being trend stationary but with at least one break in the trend. Further, could the log of this payroll employment series hypothetically be trend stationary without any breaks but the tests are making Type II errors by failing to reject the null hypothesis when it may be false?

Still, the test results to follow suggest that downward breaks in the log of total nonfarm payroll employment in the U.S. occurring either with or near the onsets of negative-aggregate-demand-shock recessions could have long-term negative consequences for subsequent growth in U.S. nonfarm payroll employment. But if that is the case, then negative-aggregate-demand-shock recessions could potentially have permanent consequences for real output growth after the recession is over unless either (1) an increase in AD occurs, (2) worker productivity increases, (3) technology improves, (4) the stock of physical capital or the supply of non-labor resources either increases or improves, or (5) some combination of these factors occurs; and the changes must be large enough to offset the impact of the earlier decrease in aggregate demand.

6.2 Breakpoint Unit Root Testing for U.S. Nonfarm Payroll Employment

Again, readers should realize that breakpoint unit root testing is not the area of my greatest expertise. In turn, they should view the following results with appropriate caution. However, I think that the results are sufficiently interesting to consider.

Given my lack of expertise, I will use breakpoint unit root testing to seek evidence for a break in the intercept of the equation for the log level of total U.S. nonfarm payroll employment. The breaks are assumed to be gradual rather than abrupt. The breakpoint unit root tests will have an intercept and a trend in the test regression equation but will have a dummy variable for a break in the intercept only. I will also use Chow (1960) breakpoint testing with the log of the payroll employment series in first difference form, testing for one or more breaks in the intercept. Would any breaks found in the intercept when the data is in 'change in the log of' form or first difference of the log of form be possible evidence of breaks in the time trend coefficient when the left-side variable is in log level form?

For breakpoint unit root testing, I use the log level of total U.S. nonfarm payroll employment on the left side of the equation. I use the method of minimizing the augmented Dickey–Fuller (1979) statistic to select the breaking month under the alternate hypothesis, and I initially use the F-statistic method for joint significance for selecting the number of lagged first differences in the log of nonfarm U.S. payroll employment to include on the right side of the regression equation. With an ADF test statistic of approximately −4.90 and an associated p-value of approximately 0.046, the test rejects the null hypothesis of a unit root in the log level of total U.S. nonfarm payroll employment at the ten percent level and the five percent level but not at the one percent level in favor of trend stationarity but with a break. The breaking month selected by minimizing the ADF was April 2007. (Recall that the total real GDP and per capita real GDP data in previous chapters were quarterly, not monthly.)

Results using the t-statistic method for selecting the number of lags are relatively similar for our purposes. Although this method selects eighteen lags of the change in the log of nonfarm payroll employment rather than twenty lags (as selected by the F-test method) and selects January 2008 as the breaking month rather than April 2007, the main results are essentially the same from our perspective. The test again produces a result that rejects the null hypothesis at the five percent level. (In fact, this trial with the t-statistic method for selecting the number of lags rejects the null hypothesis of a unit root at the one percent level.) Both trials of the test find that the time trend coefficient was statistically significant to the extent that the tests are valid. Moreover, both trials of the test find that the dummy variable for an intercept break in either April 2007 or January 2008 was statistically significant at the one percent level (to the extent that the results are valid) and that the intercept break was approximately −0.003 (roughly three tenths of one percent). Neither trial found statistically significant evidence of a temporary one-month intercept break in the year 2007 or 2008. Readers can refer to Table 6.1 for more information about the results. Some of the results from the test regression equations appear in the appendix.

The breakpoint unit root test results in Table 6.1 also include results for a trial with only six lags of the change in the log of U.S. nonfarm

Table 6.1 Breakpoint unit root test results for the natural log of total U.S. nonfarm payroll employment, January 1939 through December 2017

Lag selection method	*Statistic*	p-*Value*	*Lags*	*Break month*
F-stat joint significance	−4.891280	0.0457	20	April 2007
t-stat	−5.866171	<0.01	18	January 2008
User selected	−5.218965	0.0167	6	December 2007

Approximate critical values: 1% −5.35 5% −4.86 10% −4.61

Sources U.S. Bureau of Labor Statistics, Saint Louis Federal Reserve FRED web page, Vogelsang (1993), EViews Version 10, and the author's calculations

payroll employment. I include these results because some of the additional test results below that are not explicitly breakpoint unit root tests but rather help to conduct Chow breakpoint testing are based on equations with fewer lags, in part due to a desire for parsimony. Thus, this third breakpoint unit root test with six lags may be more similar to later Chow breakpoint tests to follow. Further, when running regressions for the change in the log of total nonfarm payroll employment as a function of a constant and lagged changes in the log of nonfarm payroll employment, starting with ten lags and eliminating the most distant lagged change in the log of payroll employment in each trial if the most distant lagged value is not significant at the ten percent level produces an equation with six lagged changes in the log of total nonfarm payroll employment. This result of six lags holds regardless of whether or not the test equation has a time trend.

In the breakpoint unit root test trial where I selected six lags, the test rejects the null hypothesis of a unit root in the log of U.S. nonfarm payroll employment at the five percent level and at the two percent level. In the test regression equation for that trial (where I selected the breaking month), the coefficient for a dummy variable representing a break in December 2007 of roughly −0.003 was statistically significant at the one percent level if valid, but the dummy variable for a one-month break in the intercept in December 2007 was not significant.

Test regression equation results in a table in the online appendix show that regression equations used for breakpoint unit root testing have coefficients for the log level of U.S. nonfarm payroll employment from one month ago greater than 0.980 but less than 0.99. In light of the fact that time series autoregressions may have a downward bias in estimating coefficients, do these estimates suggest that the natural log of total U.S. nonfarm payroll employment is either a unit root process or close to a unit root but with a break? Also note that most of the coefficients for lagged changes in the logs of the payroll employment variable from more than six months ago in the cases with eighteen and twenty lags are not significant at the five percent level or the ten percent level, even in a one-sided test.

Results not included in tables here with the user selecting seven lags also reject the null hypothesis of a unit root in the log of U.S. nonfarm payroll employment at the five percent level. Under the alternate hypothesis, the dummy variable for a downward intercept break has a coefficient of roughly −0.003 in December 2007 and was statistically significant (if valid) at the one percent level.

6.3 Chow Breakpoint Testing for U.S. Nonfarm Payroll Employment

Let's now transition to Chow (1960) breakpoint testing using payroll employment data only in 'change in the log of' form or first difference in the natural logarithm of form. We will consider tests for breaks in the intercepts of equations with data in first difference form. If breaks are found, then could that suggest breaks in time trend coefficients for the equations in log level form? In light of the facts that (1) the correlations and the covariances between the estimated residuals and the right-side time series variables appear to be essentially zero in the cases that I have checked in the equations used in Chow breakpoint testing and (2) the *first difference* of the log of total U.S. nonfarm payroll employment appears stationary in unit root testing, the results may be at least asymptotically valid if they are not valid in a finite sample period.

Given that much of the emphasis in this book is on negative aggregate demand shocks, we will search for possible evidence of breaks in the intercepts (with the data for the log of nonfarm payroll employment in first difference of the log form) either coinciding with or occurring near the beginnings of recessions as defined in this book. Before the Great Recession, the latest negative-AD-shock recession was the dot-com-bubble recession that started in the first quarter of 2001. In this section, I experimented with months near the beginnings of recessions to find where the evidence of a break in the log of nonfarm U.S. payroll employment may have been strongest. Hopefully, the experimentation trials will not affect the appropriate *p*-values much from their reported values here and in the appendix. Again, readers should interpret the results with appropriate caution.

In light of possible breaks found in the logs of both the total U.S. real GDP series and the per capita U.S. real GDP series in the previous chapter and its appendix, it may be reasonable to search for employment breaks around recessions. Results appear in the appendix for Chow breakpoint tests for single intercept breaks in equations for the change in the log of total U.S. nonfarm payroll employment. The equations differ based on (a) the number of lagged changes in the log of nonfarm payroll employment and (b) whether the hypothesized break occurred in January 1953 or May 2000. In five of the six cases, a break was found at the ten percent level, with a break at the thirteen percent level in the one exception. For more about these tests for a single break, readers should refer to the appendix.

The results in the previous subsection from breakpoint unit root testing suggest that at least one downward break in the intercept of the equation for the natural log of total U.S. nonfarm payroll employment may have occurred. Additionally, results from Chow breakpoint testing suggest that at least two possible breaks in the intercepts of equations for the change in the log of total U.S. nonfarm payroll employment, interpreted as *possible* evidence of breaks in the time trend coefficient for a version of the model with the log level of total U.S. nonfarm payroll employment as the dependent variable, also may have occurred. But, the potential for at least three breaks in U.S. nonfarm payroll employment occurring around the beginnings of negative-aggregate-demand-shock recessions suggests that decreases in aggregate demand can have either permanent or essentially permanent negative consequences for growth in employment. That could indicate the possibility of negative AD shocks having either permanent or essentially permanent deleterious implications for the growth path of real GDP for an economy. That is, hysteresis in employment could lead to hysteresis in real output.

Given the findings in the previous chapter of potentially multiple breaks in the intercepts of regression equations for the change in the log of U.S. real GDP interpreted as *possibly* suggesting breaks in the trend growth coefficient when the equation is in log level form, we also consider the possibility of two downward shifts within the same regression equation in regressions for the change in the log of U.S. nonfarm payroll employment used in this section. The equations with six lags and seven lags of the change in the log of total U.S. nonfarm payroll employment find evidence of joint breaks in the intercept in January 1953 and May 2000 at the four percent level. The equation with twenty lags finds evidence of joint breaks in those months at the eleven percent level, just missing the ten percent level based on the *F*-statistic result. The significance with twenty lags was at the ten percent level using the Wald result. Readers can see the results in Table 6.2. Future work could look for breaks in coefficients (rather than just the intercept) in univariate regressions for the change in the log of U.S. total nonfarm payroll employment.

Readers should realize that this chapter and its appendix present results from tests (breakpoint unit root tests, Chow breakpoint tests) seeking breaks in the log of U.S. nonfarm payroll employment around the times of three recessions: the recessions that started in 1953, 2001, and 2008. Results from the previous chapter found that breaks in U.S. real output could have occurred around other recessions as well. Thus, the possible breaks found in the log of nonfarm payroll *employment* may not explain all breaks in *real output* identified.

If negative AD shocks could have very long-term ramifications to the downside for real output in an economy, all other things equal, then that would likely reduce the derived demand for labor, helping us to understand slower growth in employment and slower growth in wages and salaries. Similarly, if fewer jobs are added to an economy, then that could lead to smaller gains in real output by reducing the ability to produce. However, the first line of reasoning may better help to understand one of the reasons (at least through late 2021 or early 2022) for relatively low inflation coming after relatively rapid money supply growth starting

Table 6.2 Chow breakpoint tests for two joint breaks in January 1953 and May 2000 in the intercepts of the equations for the change in the natural log of total U.S. nonfarm payroll employment

Test	*Six lags Test stat*	*p-value*	*Seven lags Test stat*	*p-value*	*Twenty lags Test stat*	*p-value*
F	3.402535	0.0337**	3.442949	0.0324**	2.306799	0.1002
Wald	6.805070	0.0333**	6.885898	0.0320**	4.613599	0.0996*

sample from January 1939 through December 2017, two asterisks (**) represent significance at the five percent level, one asterisk (*) represents significance at the ten percent level

Sources U.S. Bureau of Labor Statistics, Saint Louis Federal Reserve FRED web page, and the author's calculations

in the Great Recession. This could assume a strong relationship between nominal wage and salary increases and general price level increases in an economy.

Additionally, the COVID-19 coronavirus pandemic could have resulted in another potential break in U.S. total nonfarm payroll employment. Data from the U.S. Bureau of Labor Statistics (2022) accessed February 28, 2022 from the FRED website of the St. Louis Federal Reserve Bank and my calculations show that total U.S. nonfarm payroll employment in January 2022 was still nearly 2.9 million less than its peak in February 2020. Tests for such a break are beyond the scope of this book (at least in its current form) due in part to concern about having a sufficient number of observations to test for a break at some point in data from the year 2020. However, tests for an additional break in nonfarm payroll employment in 2020 will probably be a topic for future work and could help to guide stabilization policy decisions.

6.4 Summary of Results from Testing for Employment Breaks and Preparation for the Final Chapter

This chapter has presented results from tests for breaks in the log of nonfarm payroll employment and the change in the log of nonfarm payroll employment. Breakpoint unit root testing found evidence supporting the hypothesis that a downward break in the level of nonfarm payroll employment occurred around the start of the Great Recession. Chow breakpoint testing found evidence of two joint downward breaks in the change in the log of nonfarm payroll employment, which *could* support the view that downward breaks in the trend coefficient in the equation for the log level of nonfarm payroll employment occurred. One of these two breaks from Chow breakpoint testing was in the year 1953, and the other was in the year 2000.

Readers should realize that if downward breaks in employment occur, then not only does that reduce the ability of an economy to produce goods and services barring a sufficient improvement in technology and/or a sufficient increase in non-labor inputs (possibly and/or a sufficient increase in AD). Those who would be employed without a downward break in employment who wind up not employed due to a downward break have less ability to consume unless they have sufficient non-labor sources of income and/or wealth. Of course, this suggests that decreases in aggregate demand associated with recessions could have long-lasting implications. Also, do some recessions including AD-shock recessions sometimes lead to decreases in population growth? Readers should also remember that Chapters 3 and 5 (the former without hypothesis testing) found *possible* evidence of more than three breaks in U.S. real GDP. Because this chapter finds evidence of breaks in employment around three periods, factors other than employment may be causing recessions to be associated with downward breaks in U.S. real GDP.

Sample periods for the econometric work to this point have ended usually if not always before the year 2019. How do results from extended sample periods compare with the results presented to this point? Also, what are some explanations for the results, why are the results important, and what are some areas for future work? Those will be topics in the next chapter.

References

Chow, G. C. (1960). Tests of equality between sets of coefficients in two linear regressions. *Econometrica, 28*(3), 591–605.

Dickey, D. A., & Fuller, W. A. (1979). Distribution of the estimators for autoregressive time series with a unit root. *Journal of the American Statistical Association, 74*, 427–431.

Phillips, P. C. B., & Perron, P. (1988). Testing for a unit root in time series regression. *Biometrika, 75*, 335–346.

U.S. Bureau of Labor Statistics. (2020, 16 May). *All employees, total nonfarm [PAYEMS]*. Retrieved from FRED, Federal Reserve Bank of St. Louis. https://fred.stlouisfed.org/series/PAYEMS.

U.S. Bureau of Labor Statistics. (2022, 27 February). *All employees, total nonfarm [PAYEMS]*. Retrieved from FRED, Federal Reserve Bank of St. Louis. https://fred.stlouisfed.org/series/PAYEMS. (although the data were probably accessed February 28, 2022.

Vogelsang, T. J. (1993). Computer program (unpublished).

CHAPTER 7

Similar Results from an Extended Sample Period and Concluding Remarks to Guide Future Work

Abstract This chapter extends the sample period for some of the empirical work from earlier chapters. Many of the results presented continue to support the view that negative AD shocks can have long-lasting consequences, thus enhancing robustness. To begin to explain the importance of AD, this chapter notes that rising economic inequality could be a factor. Keynes' observation that income saved today is not necessarily spent tomorrow can help to improve our understanding. Regarding policy implications, to try to prevent downward breaks in real GDP and employment, policymakers can consider implementing fiscal policy and monetary policy more expansionary than during the recessions and recoveries of most recent recessions with the possible exception of the COVID-19 recession, where policy was relatively expansionary. A job guarantee program could lessen the loss of employment and output usually associated with downturns, as well as provide much needed income to those who otherwise would not have employment. Future work could better explain hysteresis and secular stagnation. It could also test for cointegration between real GDP, employment, and perhaps other variables but in light of possible breaks. Future work could also attempt to improve the IS-LM model.

Keywords Job guarantee program · Modern money theory · Macroeconomics · Equation of exchange · Post Keynesian school of macroeconomic thought · Employment · Breaks · Real GDP

H. C. Hartman, *Bad Breaks in Real GDP and Employment*,
https://doi.org/10.1007/978-3-031-57769-7_7

7.1 Introduction and an Extended Sample Period with a Simple Method for Estimating Trend

Readers may question whether extending the sample period beyond the second quarter of 2016, the last quarter of data for much if not most of the econometric analysis in this book, substantially changes the conclusions that one would draw. To address this issue succinctly, the answer is probably not. Work with an extended sample period could help to address the criticism that econometric models may not be very reliable out of the sample period. It would certainly help to improve the robustness of the results from shorter sample periods.

This chapter will lengthen the sample period through the fourth quarter of 2019 for some of the econometric analysis presented in Chapters 3 and 5. The real GDP data for the U.S., both in total and in per capita form, were compiled by the U.S. Bureau of Economic Analysis (2020a, 2020b) and were accessed from the Saint Louis Federal Reserve Bank FRED web page in June 2020. (Note that data values for quarters prior to the third quarter of 2016 may have been revised from their values used in the econometric work in Chapters 3, 4, and 5. Also, note that real GDP is measured in 2012-constant-buying-power chained U.S. dollars in the data for this chapter rather than in 2009-constant-buying-power chained U.S. dollars. Moreover, the next section (Sect. 7.2) presents results from breakpoint unit root testing before Chow breakpoint testing in Sect. 7.3, unlike the order in Chapter 5.) Table 7.1 displays the estimated trend coefficients and the estimated intercepts from equations for the natural logs of total U.S. real GDP and per capita U.S. real GDP with the data updated in all cases and in two of the six equations the sample period extended through the fourth quarter of 2019.

First, recall the approach from Chapter 3 which used a very simple method for estimating the trend growth path of an economy using the natural logarithm of the output variable. There are no lagged values of the log of the output variable in the estimated equations in this very simple method. When the sample period ended with the second quarter of 2016, the U.S. economy had failed to return to its estimated trend by the end of the sample period as a result of the Great Recession. This result held whether using the log of either total U.S. real GDP or per capita U.S. real GDP. The result also held whether estimating the trend using data through the second quarter of 2016 or stopping the estimation of trend with data from the fourth quarter of 2007, the last quarter in which total

Table 7.1 Estimates of the intercept and the trend coefficient in equations for the natural log of real U.S. GDP, either in total or per capita, as a function of an intercept and a time trend multiplied by a coefficient

GDP	*1947q1–2007q4 Intercept*	*Coeff*	*1947q1–2019q4 Intercept Coeff*	*2001q1–2007q4 Intercept*	*Coeff*	*Coefficient*
Total	7.674555	0.008412	7.724106	0.007854	7.898694	0.007301
Per capita	9.560025	0.005471	9.596619	0.005058	9.660015	0.004971

The sample periods for estimating trends run from (i) the first quarter of 1947 through the fourth quarter of 2007, (ii) the first quarter of 1947 through the fourth quarter of 2019, and (iii) the first quarter of 2001 through the fourth quarter of 2007. Note that 'Coeff' refers to trend coefficient
Sources U.S. Bureau of Economic Analysis, St. Louis Federal Reserve Bank FRED website, and the author's calculations

real GDP increased prior to the Great Recession, and then projecting the previous trend through the recession and the subsequent recovery. The result also held when estimating the trend only from the first quarter of 2001 (rather than the start of the sample period) through the fourth quarter of 2007 and then projecting the trend beyond the fourth quarter of 2007. As a reminder, regarding other cases for earlier recessions where the estimation of trend stopped the last quarter of the expansion immediately before the recession being analyzed for a possible return to trend, the logs of total real output and per capita real output in many though not all cases failed to return to the forward projections of their pre-recession trends prior to the start of the next recession.

Focusing now on results for the Great Recession, note that not only have the logs of total and per capita U.S. real GDP failed to return to the trends of those variables estimated with updated data (a) from the first quarter of 1947 through the fourth quarter of 2007, (b) from the first quarter of 1947 through the fourth quarter of 2019, and (c) from the first quarter of 2001 through the fourth quarter of 2007, but in each of the six cases, comparing the actual and projected values (using only the revised data for the actual and projected values) from the second quarter of 2016 with those from the fourth quarter of 2019, after the second quarter of 2016 the gap between the pre-recession trends and their actual data counterparts generally continued to grow larger! Readers may want to note that in two of the six cases referenced above, the actual real output variable was not at its largest post-Great Recession amount below its trend estimate in the fourth quarter of 2019. Those two cases were both for per capita real GDP, with one case estimating trend over the full sample period and the other from only the first quarter of 2001 through the fourth quarter of 2007.

When estimating the trend from the first quarter of 1947 through the fourth quarter of 2007, the difference between the actual natural log of total real GDP and the trend of the log of total real GDP in the fourth quarter of 2007, at around −0.053, implies that real output in the U.S. was about 5.2 per cent below its trend in that quarter. Larger shortfalls would follow. Using total U.S. real GDP with the trend estimated through the fourth quarter of 2007 and projected forward, the difference in the natural logs of actual and trend real GDP (recalling that this difference would have been a value for a 'gap variable' in Chapter 3 terminology) in the second quarter of 2016 was roughly −0.23, implying approximately a 20.3 per cent shortfall of actual real GDP below its pre-recession trend. For the fourth quarter of 2019, the natural log difference was about −0.259, corresponding with real output approximately 22.8 per cent below the estimated pre-recession trend. Note that over the fourteen additional quarters through the fourth quarter of 2019, the log of real GDP fell by nearly 2.5 additional percentage points below its pre-Great-Recession trend.

The paragraphs below focus on percentage differences between the natural log of either total U.S. real GDP or per capita U.S. real GDP and its trend. Readers can refer to Table 7.2 for 'gap variables' in natural log form.

Table 7.2 Selected estimated values of (data likely revised for) the actual natural log of real GDP minus its trend for both total U.S. real GDP and per capita U.S. real GDP (Per Cap) in the fourth quarter of 2007, the second quarter of 2016, and the fourth quarter of 2019

Qtr	*1947q1–2007q4 Total*	*Per Cap*	*1947q1–2019q4 Total*	*Per Cap*	*2001q1–2007q4 Total*	*Per Cap*
2007q4	−0.0534	−0.0296	+0.0327	+0.0342	−0.0076	−0.0081
2016q2	−0.2269	−0.1672	−0.1218	−0.0893	−0.1433	−0.1286
2019q4	−0.2587	−0.1773	−0.1459	−0.0936	−0.1596	−0.1317

More accurate estimates of the percentage differences between actual real GDP and its trend not in natural log form may appear in the text of Sect. 7.1

Sources U.S. Bureau of Economic Analysis, St. Louis Federal Reserve Bank FRED website, and the author's calculations

When the trend was estimated not through the fourth quarter of 2007 but rather through the fourth quarter of 2019, the difference between real GDP and its trend still widened between the second quarter of 2016 and the fourth quarter of 2019. With this estimate of trend, the values of the natural log of total U.S. real GDP and its trend imply that real GDP was approximately 3.3 per cent above trend rather than below trend in the fourth quarter of 2007. However, the values for the log of actual U.S. real GDP and its trend were such that in the second quarter of 2016, actual real GDP was about 11.5 per cent below trend in that quarter. The gap had widened by about two percentage points as the sample period continued, with actual U.S. real GDP about 13.6 per cent below trend in the fourth quarter of 2019.

With the trend of total U.S. real GDP estimated with data only from the first quarter of 2001 through the fourth quarter of 2007, the calculations imply that real GDP was about 0.76 per cent below its trend in the fourth quarter of 2007. By the second quarter of 2016, real GDP was about 13.4 per cent below its pre-recession trend with trend estimated over this relatively short period. The shortfall of actual U.S. real GDP below its pre-recession trend had widened to approximately 14.8 per cent in the fourth quarter of 2019 with trend estimated from 2001q1 through 2007q4.

Similar patterns emerge from analysis of per capita U.S. real GDP. When the trend was estimated from the first quarter of 1947 through the fourth quarter of 2007, the values for the natural log of U.S. per capita real GDP and its trend imply that actual per capita real U.S. GDP was about 2.92 per cent below its trend in the latter quarter. Values in subsequent quarters imply that per capita U.S. real GDP had fallen to about 15.4 per cent below its trend in the second quarter of 2016 and roughly 16.2 per cent below trend in the fourth quarter of 2019.

When estimating the trend of the log of U.S. per capita real GDP through the fourth quarter of 2019, the results suggest that per capita U.S. real GDP was about 3.5 per cent above trend in the fourth quarter of 2007. For the second quarter of 2016, per capita real GDP was about 8.5 per cent below its estimated trend, and the gap had widened to about 8.9 per cent in the fourth quarter of 2019. This is somewhat less than the shortfall of actual per capita real GDP below trend in the second quarter of 2017, when the gap was about nine per cent, the largest post-Great Recession shortfall using this estimate of trend.

By comparison, when estimating the trend of per capita real GDP with data spanning only 2001q1–2007q4, the shortfall of per capita real GDP below trend was less than one per cent, amounting to about 0.8 per cent, in the fourth quarter of 2007. The gap had increased to about 12.1 per cent below trend in the second quarter of 2016 and further widened to about 12.3 per cent in the fourth quarter of 2019. The gap with this estimate of trend per capita real GDP (in natural log form) was a bit wider in a few other post-Great Recession quarters, including a value of about 12.5 per cent in the second quarter of 2017, when the post-Great Recession gap of the log of actual per capita real GDP below its trend was the widest. Readers may want to note that both in this case with the trend of the log of per capita real GDP estimated from the first quarter of 2001 through the fourth quarter of 2007 and in the previous case with the trend estimated over the full sample period, the actual log of per capita real GDP fell further below trend in the last three quarters of the sample period, the second quarter of 2019 through the fourth quarter of 2019, despite not being at its largest post-Great Recession shortfall in the fourth quarter of 2019.

7.2 Breakpoint Unit Root Testing with an Extended Sample Period

Chapter 5 offered hypothesis tests more formal than the analysis in Chapter 3, including breakpoint unit root tests. When allowing the quarter that minimizes the augmented Dickey and Fuller (1979) statistic to be the breaking quarter under the alternate hypothesis, a breakpoint unit root test in the current chapter using data ending with the fourth quarter of 2019 (rather than the second quarter of 2016 as was the case in Chapters 3 and 5) again fails to reject the null hypothesis of a unit root in the log level of real output despite allowing for a break in one quarter under the alternate hypothesis. The *p*-value of roughly 0.72 associated with the test statistic in Table 7.3 shows that the test is not able to reject the null hypothesis at a level even close to the ten per cent level. This test used the *F*-statistic approach for selecting the number of lagged changes in the log of real output, with the approach choosing twelve lags, but the *t*-statistic approach would also select twelve lags.

The test equation had an intercept and a trend but allowed a break only in the intercept under the alternate hypothesis. If the alternate hypothesis were true, then the procedure of minimizing the augmented Dickey

Table 7.3 Selected breakpoint unit root test results for the natural log of total U.S. real GDP

End quarter	*Break quarter*	*ADF stat*	*Stat* p-*value*	*Dummy type*	*Dummy coefficient*	*Dummy* p-*value*
2019q4	2007q4	−3.462782	0.7154	Intercept	−0.009731	0.0004
				One-Time	0.008309	0.3118
2019q4	2007q4[a]	−3.462782	<0.05	Intercept	−0.009731	0.0004
				One-Time	0.008309	0.3118
2019q4	2008q1[a]	−3.297776	<0.10	Intercept	−0.009391	0.0008
				One-Time	−0.003717	0.6511

Intercept refers to an intercept dummy variable (for a permanent change in the intercept) starting in the breaking quarter, One-Time refers to a dummy variable for a temporary one-quarter change in the intercept. Both the *F*-statistic approach and the *t*-statistic approach selected twelve lagged first differences of the log of total U.S. real GDP for the test equation

Note [a]denotes the author's selection of the break date. Approximate critical values for these cases where the author selected the break date—five per cent: −3.4, ten per cent: −2.4

Sources EViews 10, Vogelsang (1993), Perron (1989), Perron and Vogelsang (1993), U.S. Bureau of Economic Analysis, St. Louis Federal Reserve Bank FRED website, and the author's calculations

and Fuller (1979) statistic would select a break in the fourth quarter of 2007, one quarter before real GDP started to decrease in the Great Recession in the U.S. based on quarterly data. The estimated coefficient for the dummy variable was approximately −0.0097, implying a downward break in U.S. real GDP of roughly one per cent. With a *p*-value less than 0.0005, the intercept break variable is statistically significant at the one per cent level, to the extent that the *t*-statistics for dummy variables like this are valid.

Does (1) the failure to reject the null hypothesis of a unit root and (2) the finding that if the alternate hypothesis were true, then an intercept break occurred at the one per cent level around the time of a decrease in aggregate demand suggest that at least one negative AD shock in the sample period had a permanent impact on the log of U.S. total real GDP? In addition to the possibility of a permanent intercept break, the test equation also allows for the possibility of a temporary one-quarter intercept break but assumed a gradual phasing in of the permanent intercept break. As shown in Table 7.3, the dummy variable for this temporary break was not statistically significant.

The use of the *t*-statistic method rather than the *F*-statistic method for selecting the number of lagged first differences in the log of real GDP produces the same results. But in both cases, the procedure of selecting the breaking quarter was minimizing the augmented Dickey and Fuller (1979) statistic. However, if I select the fourth quarter of 2007 as the breaking quarter, then the regression results appear the same and the test statistic appears the same, both when compared with the results from the test using the augmented Dickey–Fuller approach to select the breaking quarter, but with one critical difference. This second trial with the user selecting the breaking quarter rejects the null hypothesis of a unit root in the log level of real GDP in favor of trend stationarity but with a single intercept break at the five per cent level. Clearly, the difference between (1) using the break period trial with the smallest ADF statistic and (2) the user directly choosing the break period has crucial ramifications for test critical values.

Given that the estimated coefficient for the lagged change in real output from one quarter earlier is greater than 0.955 and that there could be a downward bias in the estimated coefficient, could this possibly imply that U.S. real GDP has either a unit root or a near unit root? If I specify the first quarter of 2008 as the breaking quarter and keep the other options the same, then the results for our purposes are similar to those where I chose the fourth quarter of 2007 as the breaking quarter, except that the test rejects the null hypothesis of a unit root at the ten per cent level but not at the five per cent level.

As was the case with the related material in Chapter 5, the purpose of this book is not to decide whether the natural log of real GDP is trend stationary but with a break or whether it is a unit root process. The point is that with either characterization, it is possible that at least one decrease in aggregate demand has had a long-term impact on the future growth path of real GDP in the economy.

Breakpoint unit root test results for the log of U.S. per capita real GDP over the somewhat longer sample period through the fourth quarter of 2019 also fail to reject the null hypothesis of a unit root when using (1) the ADF procedure to select the breaking quarter under the alternate hypothesis, (2) either the t-statistic method or the F-statistic method to select the number of lagged first differences of the log of per capita real output in the test equation, and (3) the innovation outlier approach for phasing in the break. As shown in Table 7.4, the p-value associated with the test statistic, at around 0.47, is not even close to the ten per cent level. The breaking quarter chosen by the ADF procedure is the fourth quarter of 2007.

Table 7.4 Selected breakpoint unit root test results for the natural log of per capita U.S. real GDP

End quarter	*Break quarter*	*ADF stat*	*Stat p-value*	*Dummy type*	*Dummy coefficient*	*Dummy p-value*
2019q4	2007q4	−3.843835	0.4725	Intercept	−0.010297	0.0002
				One-Time	0.008777	0.2873
2019q4	2007q4[a]	−3.843835	<0.025	Intercept	−0.010297	0.0002
				One-Time	0.008777	0.2873
2019q4	2008q1[a]	−3.674743	<0.05	Intercept	−0.010033	0.0003
				One-Time	−0.002643	0.7489

Intercept refers to an intercept dummy variable (for a permanent change in the intercept) starting in the breaking quarter, One-Time refers to a dummy variable for a temporary one-quarter change in the intercept. Both the F-statistic approach and the t-statistic approach selected twelve lagged first differences of the log of per capita U.S. real GDP for the test equation

Note [a]denotes the author's selection of the break date. Approximate critical values for these cases where the author selected the break date—five per cent: −3.4, ten per cent: −2.4

Sources EViews 10, Vogelsang (1993), Perron (1989), Perron and Vogelsang (1993), U.S. Bureau of Economic Analysis, St. Louis Federal Reserve Bank FRED website, and the author's calculations

However, if I specify the fourth quarter of 2007 as the breaking quarter rather than using ADF statistic minimization to select it, then the breakpoint unit root test rejects the null hypothesis of a unit root at the 2.5 per cent level in favor of the alternate hypothesis of trend stationarity with a break in the fourth quarter of 2007. The estimated coefficient for the dummy variable break implies a loss of per capita real GDP of roughly one per cent, and the dummy for this permanent break is significant at the one per cent level, if valid. Specifying the first quarter of 2008 as the breaking quarter produces rather similar results to those from specifying the fourth quarter of 2007 as the breaking quarter except that the significance level for rejecting the null hypothesis is at the five per cent level but not the 2.5 per cent level, as shown in Table 7.4.

Yet again, this book does not take a stance on whether the natural logs of per capita U.S. real GDP and total U.S. real GDP are better modeled as unit root processes or as trend stationary with breaks. The key point here is that at least one negative aggregate demand shock, the one associated with the onset of the Great Recession, may also have been associated with a permanent downward shift in the intercept of the test regression equation. Given that we have rather similar results using per capita U.S. real GDP as those produced by the use of total U.S. real GDP, the possible negative break or breaks in the intercept in the log of total U.S. real GDP probably cannot be explained only by a change or changes in population or the population growth rate. Further, possible downward breaks in per capita real GDP suggest possible losses of well-being in an economy relative to what they would have been without any downward breaks.

Readers may recall that with the sample period through the second quarter of 2016, unit root tests in the appendix found that the natural log of U.S. real GDP, both in total and per capita, concluded that both of the series have unit roots. Given these findings and the findings of others, it is likely that extending the sample period through the fourth quarter of 2019 for unit root testing without a breakpoint would also conclude that each of these two output variables has a unit root.

Perhaps as an aside, readers may have noticed that the *p*-values for the breakpoint unit root tests using the ADF minimization approach to select the breaking quarter with the sample period running through the year 2019 are lower than those from Chapter 5 with fewer observations. On the one hand, does this indicate less support in Chapter 7 results for the view that the logs of total U.S. real GDP and per capita U.S. real GDP have unit roots because the *p*-values are lower? Alternatively, does this suggest instead stronger support in this chapter results because the inclusion of more data observations in the test trials still resulted in *p*-values well above 0.10?

7.3 Chow Breakpoint Testing with an Extended Sample Period and a Brief Recap

Chapter 5 presented other tests in addition to breakpoint unit root tests, with one of the categories of tests being Chow (1960) breakpoint testing. Of the cases that I have considered with the extended sample period, Chow breakpoint tests with the sample period ending with the fourth quarter of 2019 rather than the second quarter of 2016 are at least somewhat similar to the results from Chapter 5 which had a sample period ending with the second quarter of 2016. Like Chapter 5, each of the two Chow breakpoint test regression equations for the changes in the logs of total U.S. real GDP and per capita U.S. real GDP has one lagged change in the output variable, an intercept, and an error term.

Possible evidence of single breaks and multiple breaks in the intercepts of the equations for the first differences of the natural logs of total U.S. real GDP and per capita U.S. real GDP using the longer sample period follow below, as well as evidence not as supportive of the hypothesis. The evidence is stronger in each case for at least one intercept break in the log of the total U.S. real GDP series rather than the log of per capita U.S. real GDP. Do these possible breaks in the intercepts when the data are in first difference (of the log) form indicate breaks in the trend coefficient when the data are in log level form? At any rate, the similarities of the *p*-values in this section with those from comparable tests in Chapter 5 suggest that the general conclusions about the natural log of total U.S. real GDP from Chapter 5 are likely not solely due to ending the sample period with the second quarter of 2016. However, the evidence of breaks may be stronger in the comparable Chow breakpoint tests in Chapter 5 than the ones in this chapter.

Note that results in the appendix show that all but two of the individual quarters in the table that I have tested for a single break in the change in the natural log of total U.S. real GDP in the quarters in the table find evidence of a single break in the intercept at the ten per cent level. When including some quarters that did not start a recession but were near the start of a recession, many also find evidence of a single break at the five per cent level. Regarding per capita real output, although none of the tests that I tried using a recession-initiating quarter found evidence of a break at the ten per cent level, results using the first quarter of 2001 and the first quarter of 2008 were somewhat close to the ten per cent level. Further, results for the third quarter of 2000 and the second quarter of 2006 found evidence of single breaks in those quarters either at or very close to the ten per cent level.

In terms of the possibility of multiple intercept breaks with differenced data, applying the Chow breakpoint test to the change in the log of total U.S. real GDP found evidence of multiple breaks at the ten per cent level for all of the combinations of quarters in Table 7.5. For Sets 2a, 2e, and 2f, the significance was at the five per cent level, although Sets 2e and 2f are comprised of quarters that are near the beginnings of recessions. None of the sets in Table 7.5 with the change in the log of per capita real GDP produced evidence of multiple intercept breaks at the ten per cent level. However, Set 2e found evidence of two breaks at the 13.5 per cent level, and Set 2f found evidence of two breaks at the 13 per cent level.

In summary, the extension of the sample period through the fourth quarter of 2019 could somewhat weaken the case for multiple intercept breaks from Chow breakpoint testing using data for the changes in the natural logs of total U.S. real GDP and per capita U.S. real GDP. This

Table 7.5 Chow breakpoint test results for multiple breaks in the intercepts of equations for the first difference in the natural log of either total U.S. real GDP or per capita U.S. real GDP using the indicated sets of quarters

Set	*Quarters*	*d.o.f*	*Model A values* F-*test*	*Wald*	*Model B values* F-*test*	*Wald*
Set 1	01q1 + 08q1	(2, 286)	0.0706*	0.0688*	0.2817	0.2801
Set 2	Set 1 + 53q3	(3, 285)	0.0589*	0.0567*	0.3083	0.3063
Set 3	Set 1 + 73q3	(3, 285)	0.0692*	0.0669*	0.3811	0.3794
Set 4	Set 2 + 73q3	(4, 284)	0.0846*	0.0816*	0.4423	0.4407
Set 2a	53q3 + 01q1	(2, 286)	0.0300**	0.0287**	0.1832	0.1813
Set 2e	53q2 + 00q3	(2, 286)	0.0190**	0.0180**	0.1320	0.1301
Set 2f	53q2 + 06q2	(2, 286)	0.0192**	0.0182**	0.1285	0.1266

Sample period from the first quarter of 1947 through the fourth quarter of 2019. The first number under 'd.o.f.' before the comma gives the degrees of freedom associated with the Wald statistic *p*-value for the set in that row. Note that a single asterisk (*) denotes significance at the ten per cent level, while two asterisks (**) represent significance at the five per cent level

Set 1 has quarters 2001q1 and 2008q1

Set 2 has quarters 1953q3, 2001q1, and 2008q1

Set 3 has quarters 1973q3, 2001q1, and 2008q1

Set 4 has quarters 1953q3, 1973q3, 2001q1, and 2008q1

Set 2a has quarters 1953q3 and 2001q1

Set 2e has quarters 1953q2 and 2000q3

Set 2f has quarters 1953q2 and 2006q2

Sources U.S. Bureau of Economic Analysis, St. Louis Federal Reserve Bank FRED website, and the author's calculations

may be particularly true for the per capita data, where no combination that I have tried found evidence at the ten per cent level of multiple intercept breaks for the change in the log of per capita U.S. real GDP, although Sets 2e and 2f were somewhat close. However, after extending the sample period through the fourth quarter of 2019, the case may be somewhat stronger for the natural logs (in log level, un-differenced form) of total U.S. real GDP and per capita U.S. real GDP failing to return to their pre-recession trends following the Great Recession when using a simple method for estimating the trend, the method from Chapter 3.

Expanding the sample period through the fourth quarter of 2019 did not seem to make much difference in results from breakpoint unit root testing in terms of failing to reject the null hypothesis of a unit root when using the ADF method to select the breaking quarter. It may be notably less likely that the log of the per capita U.S. real GDP series has a unit root when allowing for a possible intercept break in the fourth quarter of 2007 (where I chose the fourth quarter of 2007 as the breaking quarter) with the extended sample period, where the rejection of the null hypothesis of a unit root is at the 2.5 per cent level rather than the five per cent level. Maybe I should emphasize that the possible permanent downward break found in the per capita series, the fourth quarter of 2007, is approximately when a decrease in aggregate demand occurred. Given the possibilities of (1) an intercept break in the log of per capita U.S. real GDP from breakpoint unit root testing and (2) at least one intercept break, particularly when ending the sample period with the second quarter of 2016, in the first difference of the log of per capita real GDP from Chow breakpoint testing (which may *possibly* indicate a break in the trend coefficient with the data in log level form), possible breaks in the log of total U.S. real GDP may not be fully explained by changes in either the population or the population growth rate. Readers should realize that I do not include as many sets of quarters in Table 7.5 as I did in comparable tables in Chapter 5.

7.4 Book Summary to This Point

This work has presented evidence largely supporting but sometimes contradicting the view that negative shocks can have longer term consequences for real output and employment. In contrast to mainstream macroeconomic theory as it stood recently if not presently, this work finds that *at least some negative aggregate demand shocks* in the U.S. have had a longer term impact on U.S. real GDP and U.S. employment.

Following a literature review in Chapters 1 and 2 on the major schools of macroeconomic thought and on the permanence of negative aggregate demand shocks and some related econometric studies, Chapter 3 offered a very simple method for estimating the trend of the natural log of U.S. real GDP, both in total and in per capita form. Negative AD shocks such as the collapse of the dot com bubble and the securitized debt financial crisis, resulted in U.S. real GDP falling below its pre-recession trend and then failing to return to the pre-recession projected trend. Not only was this true for some negative AD shocks, but it was also true for at least some negative AS shocks. If accurate, these findings substantially undermine the view that real output oscillates around an essentially unchanging upward-sloping trend and question the view that cyclical fluctuations are symmetric so that after an economy exceeds an unchanging trend, the amounts by which real output exceeds trend balance out against the amounts by which real output is below trend. Therefore, ignoring time value of money issues, business cycles may have no long-term negative net impact if real GDP fluctuated around an unchanging trend, a view that this book clearly questions.

Among other things, Chapters 4 and 5 pointed out possible shortcomings in the econometric analysis in Chapter 3. Given concerns about those potential shortcomings, Chapter 5 used more advanced (though not necessarily the most advanced) econometric techniques including using data in first difference form (or change in form), conducting Chow (1960) breakpoint testing, and breakpoint unit root testing. An advantage of the approach used in Chapter 3 is that the method and the results are probably much easier to comprehend. However, although we cannot have complete confidence in the results due to reasons noted, we can place more confidence in the results supporting the view that negative aggregate demand shocks can have long-term negative ramifications in both Chapters 3 and 5 due to the approaches in Chapters 4 and 5.

Chow (1960) breakpoint test results found that multiple breaks in the U.S. real output series may have occurred. Multiple joint breaks within the same trial may have occurred in the third quarter of 1953, the first quarter of 2001, and the first quarter of 2008. Decreases in aggregate demand likely caused all three of those recessions. Other combinations of quarters may also have produced multiple joint breaks. Further, Wald restriction tests and t-tests produced evidence of at least one break. Given that at least one break may also have occurred in the log of U.S. per capita real GDP, changes in the U.S. population or the U.S. population growth rate may not be the only explanation for the results. The only tests conducted in Chapter 5 where I did not find evidence of a break in the natural log of real output in any test trial were the Chow forecast tests.

Chapter 5 also presented breakpoint unit root test results for the log of U.S. real GDP in total and per capita. Depending on different assumptions, Chapter 5 offers some test results over the sample period ending with the second quarter of 2016 where U.S. real output (either total or per capita) is trend stationary but with one break and other test results where U.S. real output is a unit root. In cases where U.S. real output is trend stationary with a break, the dummy variable for a downward break is statistically significant if valid. With the ADF statistic selecting the break, the break occurs around the beginning of the Great Recession, associated with a negative AD shock. Whether U.S. real output is better described as trend stationary but with at least one break or a true unit root, at least one negative AD shock occurred that had a permanent impact on U.S. real output.

Additionally, Chapter 6 presented evidence of breaks in the natural log of U.S. nonfarm payroll employment. The possible decreases in both the slope and the intercept of the trend line for the log of U.S. nonfarm employment could have been associated with some of the potential breaks in U.S. real GDP. Could hysteresis in employment and other factors lead to hysteresis in real output?

The current chapter offered results from using some methods discussed in earlier chapters but with a sample period extended through the fourth quarter of 2019. That was the last quarter before U.S. real GDP started plunging due to the COVID-19 shutdowns, possibly associated with another break, as was the decline in real GDP in early 2022. Chow (1960) breakpoint test results still supported the view that downward breaks in the change in the log of U.S. real GDP occurred around the times of negative-AD-shock recessions, although the results were perhaps less supportive than those from Chapter 5. Breakpoint unit root tests in the current chapter reiterated the conclusion that the logs of U.S. total real GDP and U.S. per capita real GDP either have unit roots or are trend stationary with at least one break, perhaps somewhat more likely to conclude the latter compared with Chapter 5 results. Regarding the 'gap variable' approach of Chapter 3, the passage of additional time without real output returning to pre-recession trend (with the *possible* exception of returning to the pre-COVID-19 recession trend) may strengthen the conclusion that recessions including negative-AD-shock recessions can have essentially permanent consequences.

7.5 Thoughts about the Importance of and Explanations for the Results and Future Work

The failure of economies in the U.S. and other countries to return to pre-recession trends following at least a few recessions, including some due to negative aggregate demand shocks, has important implications. It also warrants additional study in terms of causes and consequences.

When a downward break occurs with a downward shift in the intercept of the trend line or a decrease in the slope of the trend line (assuming that real GDP data are in natural log form), an unfortunate consequence is that real GDP will not be as high as it would have been had a break in trend not occurred. Such an economy will have fewer goods and services to distribute than it would have had without the decrease in the intercept or the slope of the trend line. Readers should note that when downward breaks in the trend line occur around the times of recessions, it remains likely that the economy will produce more at some point after the recession ends than the economy produced before the recession began. But the key point is that had no downward break occurred, the economy would have wound up producing *even more*. As a consequence, at least some people in the economy will not be able to consume as many goods and services as the quantities of goods and services that they would have been able to enjoy had the economy returned to trend.

Given that resources are finite but wants are virtually unlimited, think of all of the wants and unfortunately in some cases needs that could have been satisfied had economies been able to return to their pre-recession trends following all recessions. Tragically, in some cases, basic nutrition and adequate shelter could be two of the goods that people would have had in greater quantities if growth had been stronger by returning real output to trend. But even in cases less dire, think about all of the goods and services that could have been produced and consumed had real output growth been greater. To the extent that the results from Chapter 3 are valid, they suggest that following at least some recessions, U.S. real output would have been at least a few percentage points greater had the U.S. economy been able to return to its pre-recession trend. Consider all of the additional goods and services that people in the U.S. could have consumed if their incomes measured in constant-buying-power dollars had been a few percentage points greater most if not all years of their lives.

What may be preventing real output from returning to its pre-recession trend following at least some recessions? Further, how can economic analysis and policy incorporate the finding that some negative AD shocks may have essentially permanent negative consequences to improve macroeconomic performance and living standards for millions of people, maybe more?

Inequality could be an important factor. Unlike many works in economics that assume either no impact of increasing economic inequality on economic growth or a positive impact of rising inequality on growth, Boushey (2019) and some others find that rising inequality harms economic growth. Perhaps in addition to explanations in Boushey (2019), how is it that rising economic inequality can result in slower economic growth.

According to Keynes (1964, pp. 210–211), a unit of currency not spent in the current period does not guarantee that this particular unit of currency saved currently will be spent in the next period. For example, a U.S. dollar saved today is *not* necessarily a U.S. dollar spent tomorrow. Readers should consider the impact of an increase in the savings rate on the velocity of the money stock. Does an increase in the savings rate, all other things equal, lead to a decrease in the velocity of money? Recall that the velocity of money refers to the number of times on average that a unit of currency trades per time period in a transaction counted as a part of real output.

Refer back to Chapters 1 and 2 for a review of the velocity of money and the equation of exchange. Readers may recall that classical macroeconomics viewed the velocity of money as being nearly constant in the short term in most cases. Under this assumption, the classical interpretation of the quantity theory of money in its most extreme form suggests that increases in the money supply have no impact on real output, so that increases in the money supply lead to proportional increases in the price level. By contrast, the monetarist school of thought interpreted the quantity theory of money as having the velocity of money being predictable to a high degree (even) in the short term. With this interpretation, monetarism in most cases if not all cases argued for relatively small, predictable increases in the money supply. Monetarists believed that this would result in small, predictable increases in the price level. They may have also believed that monetary policy consistent with small predictable increases in the money stock would not spark relatively high inflation, which could wind up leading to recessions.

By an even larger contrast, economists in the Keynesian school at least implicitly assumed that the velocity of money was not constant and was not necessarily predictable. What if money velocity was not constant but was more predictable than Keynesian economists assumed but less predictable than monetarists assumed? Although money velocity is probably unpredictable to an extent, to the extent that money velocity is predictable, policymakers could potentially use forecasts of money velocity to improve the effectiveness of monetary policy. The thinking is that by explicitly using forecasts of velocity, monetary policymakers could improve their forecasts of nominal GDP. Hartman (2015) offers information about how the money supply growth rate may have a substantial impact on whether money velocity is increasing or decreasing.

Based on the possibility that U.S. nonfarm payroll employment may not return to an essentially unchanging trend following all recessions, *including some of the recessions caused by decreases in aggregate demand*, we may question whether people have misinterpreted the failure of the *unemployment rate* to drift higher essentially permanently. Assuming that the natural log of U.S. nonfarm payroll employment is either trend stationary *with at least one break* or a true unit root process, the inability of nonfarm payroll employment to return to its pre-recession growth path following at least some recessions suggests that the shortfall is likely to continue for the foreseeable future unless something changes. Should monetary policy and fiscal policy focus more on job creation?

Of the schools of macroeconomic thought, this book perhaps fits best into the post Keynesian school of thought, but with at least one possible exception. While this book assumes some degree (although less than in monetarism, classical analysis, and neoclassical analysis) of predictability to the velocity of money including the velocity of the M1 monetary aggregate, to my knowledge the post Keynesian school of thought does not necessarily assume any predictability in money velocity. The same also holds to my knowledge for the new Keynesian school. Additionally, to my knowledge, post Keynesian macroeconomic analysis may not explicitly mention the velocity of money on a frequent basis. A major area of overlap in this book and the post Keynesian school of thought would be in terms of the possibility of an insufficiency of aggregate demand resulting in the failure to reach full employment, particularly in the absence of expansionary policy. Hysteresis represents another area of commonality between the work in this book and post Keynesian macroeconomic theory. I plan to include more about how economic inequality, velocity, and other factors can potentially explain the disappointing performance of the U.S. economy over the last fifty years or so in my next book.

At least some in the post Keynesian school of macroeconomic thought, for example, Minsky according to Wray (2016, pp. 72–73), have been critical of the IS-LM model. Can the IS-LM model be improved to better understand business cycle fluctuations?

Also, the results that I have found at this point may possibly suggest that more downward breaks in the U.S. total real GDP series have occurred than in the nonfarm payroll employment series. If this result holds after further work, then do we need to rethink the relationship between employment and real GDP? For those not familiar, loosely speaking, two or more variables are cointegrated if each of the variables has a unit root (or is difference stationary) but a linear combination of them is a stationary series. A cointegrating equation is often interpreted as a long-term equilibrium relationship between the cointegrated variables. Are U.S. real GDP and U.S. nonfarm payroll employment cointegrated? Are they cointegrated with other macroeconomic variables, and do breaks change the analysis?

How may the findings that both real GDP and nonfarm payroll employment in the U.S. may suffer essentially permanent negative consequences from at least some decreases in aggregate demand guide policymakers? If negative AD shocks can potentially have long-lasting deleterious consequences for real GDP and employment, then policymakers should consider policies more expansionary than those implemented following most of the recessions that have occurred, at least in recent decades.

A possible noteworthy exception is the recession associated with the COVID-19 shutdown. With data from the U.S. Bureau of Economic Analysis (2023) found on the website of the St. Louis Federal Reserve Bank that I accessed August 18, 2023, I estimate that using the method in Chapter 3 for determining trend from the first quarter of 2008 through the fourth quarter of 2019, the natural log of total U.S. real GDP returned to its pre-recession trend following the COVID-19-associated recession and remained above trend most quarters thereafter through the second quarter of 2023 and perhaps beyond. Although this recession may have been different due to the relatively short-term shutdowns and perhaps due to the relatively rapid reopening, is it mere coincidence that (1) both fiscal policy and monetary policy tended to be *much* more expansionary than normal following recessions such as the Great

Recession and (2) U.S. real GDP had at least a temporary return to its pre-recession trend following the COVID-19 recession but U.S. real GDP never completely recovered following the Great Recession? Perhaps I should emphasize that *a major reason* why the U.S. economy returned to its pre-recession trend in this case was the *slow growth* in U.S. real GDP 2008q1–2019q4. I estimate that annual U.S. real GDP growth in that period (ignoring compounding) was less than 1.6 per cent per year. By contrast, using a growth rate of about 2.3 per cent per year, the approximate annual growth rate (ignoring compounding) from the first quarter of 2001 through the fourth quarter of 2007, U.S. real GDP probably has yet to return the trajectory from applying that growth rate starting with the COVID-19 recession in the first quarter of 2020. Moreover, with trend estimated from the first quarter of 1947 through the second quarter of 2023, U.S. total real GDP clearly failed to return to trend by the second quarter of 2023. In fact, with this estimate of trend, U.S. real GDP *never* returned to this estimate of trend after the Great Recession and, at least through 2023q2, was *further below* trend after the recession of 2020 than in the fourth quarter of 2019.

If recessions are costly from a long-term perspective, then economic policy should try to (a) prevent recessions and (b) reduce the harm done by unavoidable recessions. More expansionary policies could help. However, perhaps the policies should be implemented strategically to achieve 'the biggest bang for the buck' and to keep the federal debt-to-GDP ratio at sustainable levels.

Future work could address why negative-AD-shock recessions could be associated with downward breaks in employment. Could people decide to leave the labor force around the times of recessions due to earlier retirements? This could support the view that the growth rate of the demand for labor, a derived demand, could decrease on a more permanent basis following some recessions. Could the labor force participation rate fall due in part to skills failing to keep up with employer demands when former employees are out of work for a while? Could recessions at least sometimes be associated with decreases in fertility that lead to essentially permanent losses of population and employment? While decreases in the growth rate of labor clearly have aggregate *supply* implications, they could also have aggregate *demand* implications. With fewer employees and/or fewer people employed fully (for example, an increase in part-time employment for those who would rather work full-time), *aggregate demand growth* in the economy suffers. Given that until either 2021 or

2022, inflation in the U.S. has been fairly well contained for decades, despite rapid increases in the money stock, growth in aggregate demand has been disappointing.

Policymakers should also *consider* implementing a job guarantee program, where the federal government would act as an employer of last resort, as recommended by modern money theory, also known as modern monetary theory. Clearly, *further study would be needed* before concluding that policymakers should *adopt* a job guarantee (JG) program. One of the benefits of a JG program is that when layoffs increase and when new job market entrants are more likely to have difficulty finding work, both more likely around the times of economic downturns, job seekers could find productive employment through the job guarantee program. My understanding is that workers employed through the JG program would work to provide services needed at the community level and receive more income than under unemployment insurance. Additionally, people working in the job guarantee program would be free to leave the job guarantee program for job opportunities in the private for-profit sector and presumably also the private non-profit sector and the public sector if other employment opportunities outside of the job guarantee program would offer better pay and/or would otherwise be more attractive for employees. The JG program could help to develop skills and keep skills current for people working in such a program, perhaps making workers more attractive to non-job-guarantee employers. For more about the JG program, see Tcherneva (2020), Kelton (2020), and Wray (2015).

Structured in this way, the job guarantee program appears to be capable of serving as a price floor on labor services, which seems to be a goal of modern money theory. Such a job floor would lessen the loss of incomes usually associated with recessions and hopefully reduce the loss of real GDP and jobs during recessions. A JG program would likely reduce economic inequality, which could be one of the factors most responsible for slowing economic growth in recent decades. By giving households the opportunity to earn more incomes through the job guarantee program during tougher times and be able to spend more, creating more job opportunities outside of the job guarantee program, perhaps the U.S. and other countries could buoy aggregate demand and avoid bad breaks.

References

Boushey, H. (2019). *Unbound: How inequality constricts our economy and what we can do about it*. Harvard University Press.

Chow, G. C. (1960). Tests of equality between sets of coefficients in two linear regressions. *Econometrica, 28*(3), 591–605.

Dickey, D. A., & Fuller, W. A. (1979). Distribution of the estimators for an autoregressive time series with a unit root. *Journal of the American Statistical Association, 74*, 427–431.

Hartman, H. C. (2015). *It's velocity, stupid! Is the velocity of money the forgotten variable of macroeconomics?* Infinity Publishing.

Kelton, S. (2020). *The deficit myth: Modern monetary theory and the birth of the people's economy*. Public Affairs.

Keynes, J. M. (1964). *The general theory of employment, interest, and money*. Harcourt (original publication in 1936 by Macmillan).

Perron, P. (1989). The great crash, the oil price shock, and the unit root hypothesis. *Econometrica, 57*(6), 1361–1401.

Perron, P., & Vogelsang, T. J. (1993). The great crash, the oil price shock, and the unit root hypothesis: Erratum. *Econometrica, 61*(1), 248–249.

Tcherneva, P. R. (2020). *The case for a job guarantee*. Polity Press.

U.S. Bureau of Economic Analysis. (2020a, June 27). Real Gross Domestic Product [GDPC1], retrieved from FRED, Federal Reserve Bank of St. Louis. https://fred.stlouisfed.org/data/GDPC1.txt

U.S. Bureau of Economic Analysis. (2020b, June 27). Real Gross Domestic Product per capita [A939RX0Q048SBEA], retrieved from FRED, Federal Reserve Bank of St. Louis. https://fred.stlouisfed.org/data/A939RX0Q048SBEA.txt

U.S. Bureau of Economic Analysis. (2023, August 18). Real Gross Domestic Product [GDPC1], retrieved from FRED, Federal Reserve Bank of St. Louis. https://fred.stlouisfed.org/data/GDPC1.txt.

Vogelsang, T. J. (1993). Computer program (unpublished).

Wray, L. R. (2015). *Modern money theory: A primer on macroeconomics for sovereign monetary systems* (2nd ed.). Palgrave Macmillan.

Wray, L. R. (2016). *Why Minsky matters: An introduction to the work of a maverick economist*. Princeton University Press.

Index

A
Aggregate demand, 2–4, 6, 8, 9, 12–28, 43, 47, 48, 53–57, 60, 65, 78, 79, 83, 88, 93, 96, 97, 99, 102, 103, 106, 113–115, 119, 120, 122, 124–127
Aggregate supply, 3, 6, 13, 14, 16, 17, 22–26, 28, 48, 49, 54, 55, 126
Augmented Dickey Fuller unit root tests, 63, 65, 66, 69, 88, 98
Autocorrelation. *See* Serial correlation

B
Breakpoint unit root testing, 86, 87, 89, 91–93, 98–101, 103, 108, 119, 120
Breaks, 2, 10, 24, 38, 39, 43, 45, 47–49, 60, 63, 65, 67, 69, 72–78, 82–85, 87, 88, 91–93, 96–100, 102–106, 116–122, 125–127
Business cycles/Cyclical fluctuations, 66, 120

C
Chow breakpoint test, 63, 66, 72, 84, 85, 87, 101, 103, 104, 116, 117
Chow forecast test, 84, 87, 92
Classical school of macroeconomic thought, 3, 13, 14
Consistent estimates, 62
Consumption, 6, 23, 24, 56
COVID19 recession, 32, 53, 56, 121, 125, 126

D
Demand for labor, 96, 104, 126
Derived demand, 78, 96, 104, 126

E
Economic inequality, 88, 123, 124, 127
Employer of last resort, 127
Employment, 2, 5, 6, 8, 10, 14–17, 20, 21, 93, 97–106, 119, 121, 124–127
Equation of exchange, 13, 14, 123

H. C. Hartman, *Bad Breaks in Real GDP and Employment*,
https://doi.org/10.1007/978-3-031-57769-7

Expansionary policy, 18, 21, 124

F

Filtered variables, 9, 48
Fiscal policy, 6, 18, 20, 21, 92, 124, 125
Fitted value, 80
F Statistic. *See* F Test
F Test, 61, 62, 66, 74, 75, 100, 118

G

Gap variable, 34–38, 40, 43–45, 49, 52–55, 57, 110, 121
Generalized least squares, 63
Government purchases, 6
Gross Domestic Product (GDP), 2–5, 7, 8, 10, 12–24, 26–28, 32–58, 60, 62, 64, 65, 67, 69, 72–80, 82, 85–93, 96, 97, 100, 103, 106, 108–122, 124–127
Gross National Product, 5, 23

H

Heteroskedasticity, 61
Hypothesis testing, 2, 9, 12, 60, 61, 64–66, 69, 72, 106
Hysteresis, 21, 24, 78, 103, 121

I

Inference, Statistical, 2, 61, 90
Inflation, 3, 7, 16–19, 27, 46–48, 104, 123, 127
Interest rates, 3, 4, 6, 13, 17–19, 24
Investment, 18, 24
IS-LM Model, 125

J

Job guarantee program, 127

K

Keynesian school of macroeconomic thought, 7, 12, 15

L

L-Shaped recessions, 26

M

Markov switching, 25, 26
Method for selecting lags in breakpoint unit root testing, 100
Modern money theory, 127
Monetarist school of macroeconomic thought, 7
Monetary policy, 6, 18, 20, 48, 56, 123–125
Money, 7, 8, 13–15, 17–20, 64, 96, 104, 120, 123, 124, 127
Money Supply and Money Demand, 19

N

Negative AD shock (recession), 3, 4, 10, 12, 27, 47, 54–56, 72, 81, 83, 91, 103, 104, 113, 119–121, 123, 125
Negative AS shock (recession), 10, 56, 120
Neoclassical school of macroeconomic thought, 12
New Keynesian school of macroeconomic thought, 12, 21
Normally distributed errors, 61

O

Other Countries, 2, 3, 10, 15, 122, 127
Ordinary least squares, 62, 63, 68

Original Keynesian Aggregate Supply/ Aggregate Demand Model, 6, 14, 16

P

Phillips curve, 16
Phillips Perron unit root tests, 69, 97
Population and population growth rate, 2, 40, 77, 93, 116, 119, 120
Post-Keynesian school of macroeconomic thought, 21, 27, 124, 125
Price levels, 3, 4, 7, 13–19, 46, 96, 105, 123
Productivity, 25, 97, 99
p-values, 68, 76, 81, 82, 84, 90, 103, 116, 117

Q

Quantity theory of money, 13–15, 20, 123

R

Recession, 2, 3, 9, 10, 12, 16, 18–20, 25, 26, 32, 33, 38, 39, 43, 44, 47–57, 60, 65, 72, 73, 75, 76, 79, 80, 83, 84, 87–89, 96, 97, 99, 102–104, 106, 109, 117, 120–127
Recession of 1949, 54, 57
Recession of 1953 and 1954, 55, 57
Recession of 1956 to 1958, 57
Recession of 1959 and 1960, 55, 57
Recession of 1969 and 1970, 24, 55, 57
Recession of 1973 to 1975, 55, 57
Recession of 1980 to 1982, 57
Recession of 1990 and 1991, 27, 49, 50, 57
Regression assumptions, Standard, 61, 68, 78, 79, 82, 83, 90, 98
Residuals, 61–64, 68, 77–79, 82, 98, 102
Resource availability, 56

S

Saving, 23, 24, 123
Secular stagnation, 24
Serial correlation, 56, 61–64, 66, 69, 79, 83, 84
Spurious regression, 61, 62, 65

T

Technology, 8, 15, 18, 40, 56, 97, 99
Tests for a single break, 72, 73, 103
Tests for multiple breaks or joint breaks, 120
The Dot-Com-Bubble recession, 32, 33, 38, 39, 44, 46–49, 51–54, 58, 102
The Great Depression, 4, 15
The Great Recession, 27, 32, 33, 36, 38–40, 43, 44, 46–49, 51–58, 60, 72, 89, 90, 93, 96, 102, 105, 108, 109, 113, 115, 118, 121, 126
Transfer payments, 7
Trend, 2–5, 9, 10, 12, 16, 18, 21–25, 27, 32–58, 60, 65, 66, 72, 78, 85–88, 91, 93, 96–103, 105, 108–112, 114, 115, 117–126
Trend stationary, 9, 22–24, 85, 88, 91, 93, 98, 99, 114, 115, 121, 124
Trend stationary with breaks, 23, 115
t Statistic. *See* t Test
t Test, 78–80, 83, 84, 120
Type I errors, 78
Type II errors, 99

U

Unemployment, 5, 6, 8, 14, 16, 17, 19, 21, 97, 124, 127

Unit root or difference stationary, 9, 22–24, 56, 63–67, 69, 85–93, 97–105, 108, 112–116, 119–121, 124, 125

U-Shaped recessions, 26

U6 Unemployment rate, 97

U3 Unemployment rate, 97

V

Velocity, 13, 15, 19, 20, 123, 124

W

Wald test, 75, 80, 82

GPSR Compliance

The European Union's (EU) General Product Safety Regulation (GPSR) is a set of rules that requires consumer products to be safe and our obligations to ensure this.

If you have any concerns about our products, you can contact us on ProductSafety@springernature.com

In case Publisher is established outside the EU, the EU authorized representative is:

Springer Nature Customer Service Center GmbH
Europaplatz 3
69115 Heidelberg, Germany

The manufacturer's authorised representative in the EU is Springer Nature Customer Service Centre GmbH, Europaplatz 3, 69115 Heidelberg, Germany. If you have any concerns regarding our products, please contact ProductSafety@springernature.com

Printed and bound by CPI Group (UK) Ltd, Croydon, CR0 4YY
06/10/2026
02225878-0001